HER
RISE
HER
RULES

Praise for *Her Rise Her Rules*

"Heidi Hartman is the Queen Bee of our community's Heart Hive. Whether she is chairing the United Way's 'Women United' affinity group, mentoring young professionals, or giving her famous four-second hug at just the right time, Heidi is all-in. And anyone in her positivity path is stronger because of her energy. This book shares some of our hive's favorite 'Heidi-isms' and will have you 'noodling' about your future with a belief that tomorrow can be better than today. More importantly, you'll gain the will and the clarity toward the direction that's right for you. Just know that she and many others are in your hive and in your corner - but she'll also gently push you out of your corner."

Alison Anthony, President & CEO Tulsa Area United Way

"*Her Rise Her Rules* is a game-changer for any woman looking to not only succeed but *thrive*. It's more than just a guide; it's a mentor in your corner, offering invaluable wisdom on embracing failure as a stepping stone, cultivating a growth mindset that shatters limitations, and, building a tribe of like-minded individuals who lift you higher.

As a woman in leadership, I've often felt the pressure to be perfect, to have all the answers. This book liberates you from that impossible standard. It teaches you that failure isn't a reflection of your worth, but a crucial part of the journey to success. The concept of a growth mindset isn't just a buzzword here; it's a practical, actionable framework that empowers you to continuously learn, adapt, and expand your capabilities.

What truly sets this book apart is its emphasis on the power of community. It underscores the importance of surrounding yourself with people who not only support your professional ambitions but also nourish your personal growth. It's a reminder that we don't have to climb the ladder alone; in fact, we're stronger, more resilient, and more likely to succeed when we have a strong network of allies.

This book is a must-read for any woman who is ready to embrace her full potential, lead with authenticity, and build a life that is both successful and deeply fulfilling."

Rose Ann Garza, CHRO Kerbey Lane

"I highlight key messages in books I read. *Her Rise Her Rules* is now almost completely yellow. Hartman does what other leadership books do not. She provides practical reflections and applications to take concepts to actions and realities. A must read."

**Stephanie Cipolla, Chief Human Resources Officer
at Cherokee Nation Businesses**

7 Secrets of Successful Leaders

HER RISE HER RULES

HEIDI HARTMAN

INDIE BOOKS
INTERNATIONAL

HER RISE HER RULES
7 Secrets Of Successful Leaders

No part of this publication may be reproduced or distributed in any form or by any means without the prior permission of the publisher. Requests for permission should be directed to permissions@indiebooksintl.com or mailed to Permissions, Indie Books International, 2511 Woodlands Way, Oceanside, CA 92054.

The views and opinions in this book are those of the author at the time of writing this book and do not reflect the opinions of Indie Books International or its editors.

Neither the publisher nor the author is engaged in rendering legal or other professional services through this book. If expert assistance is required, the services of appropriate professionals should be sought. The publisher and the author shall have neither liability nor responsibility to any person or entity with respect to any loss or damage caused directly or indirectly by the information in this publication.

The Female Leadership Success Code™ is a pending trademark of Heidi Hartman.

JIF is a trademark of The J.M. Smucker Company.

Starbucks is a trademark of the Starbucks Corporation.

ISBN 13: 978-1-966168-30-0
Library of Congress Control Number: 2025911855

Original cover concept by Jessica TeRuki
Designed by Melissa Farr, Back Porch Creative, LLC

INDIE BOOKS INTERNATIONAL®, INC.
2511 WOODLANDS WAY
OCEANSIDE, CA 92054
www.indiebooksintl.com

Contents

PART I

The Leadership Success Challenge For Women

1

Why Female Leadership Under-Representation Matters

You may encounter many defeats, but you must not be defeated.

MAYA ANGELOU, POET

D ecades of research and studies show that women leaders help increase productivity, enhance fairness, and improve collaboration. Knowing this, why are there not more women in higher levels of leadership?

When more women are in leadership roles, organizations experience a direct correlation to organizational improvement and growth. Research also shows that companies with more women in leadership have greater innovation, healthier cultures, and stronger performance.

An old advertisement slogan touts that, "We've come a long way, baby." I would add that we have a long way to go. At a time when companies should be doubling down on their efforts, indications show just the opposite.

Women make up more than half of the US population, at 50.5 percent. Yet, according to a McKinsey & Company study from 2024, women are significantly underrepresented, starting at the senior manager/director level up to the C-suite level. The C-suite level includes CEO, CFO, CHRO, CMO, CAO, and CIO positions. Examples of C-Suite definitions are: Chief Human Resources Officer (CHRO), Chief Marketing Officer (CMO), Chief Administrative Officer/ Chief Accounting Officer (CAO), and/or the Chief Information Officer (CIO).

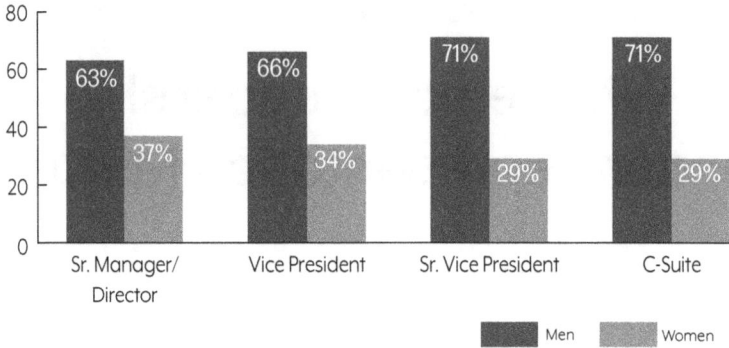

The director level feeds placement up the chain to the C-suite opportunities. This same study found that women were still just as driven for career growth at these levels but on their own terms.

At the current rate of progress, it will take almost fifty years for women in corporate America to reach parity. That is if companies in the US continue substantial efforts and progress in this area.[1]

The research bears out that performance bias exists throughout organizations. Men are typically promoted based on their perceived potential, while women are typically promoted based on what they have already accomplished.[2] Further breakdown by McKinsey Study (numbers are rounded).

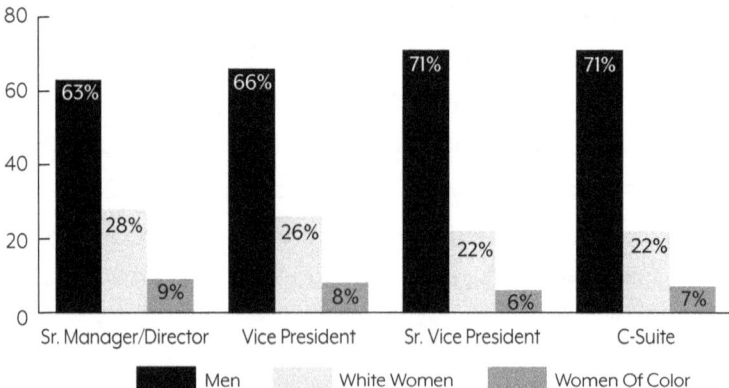

In 2023, thirty-seven of the top fifty companies' CEOs were white men. In 2023, the CEOs of the top fifty Fortune 500 companies included six white women, one Hispanic/Latino man, one Hispanic/Latino woman, three South Asian men, one black man, and one black woman.[3]

A further breakdown by the McKinsey study can be seen below (numbers are rounded):

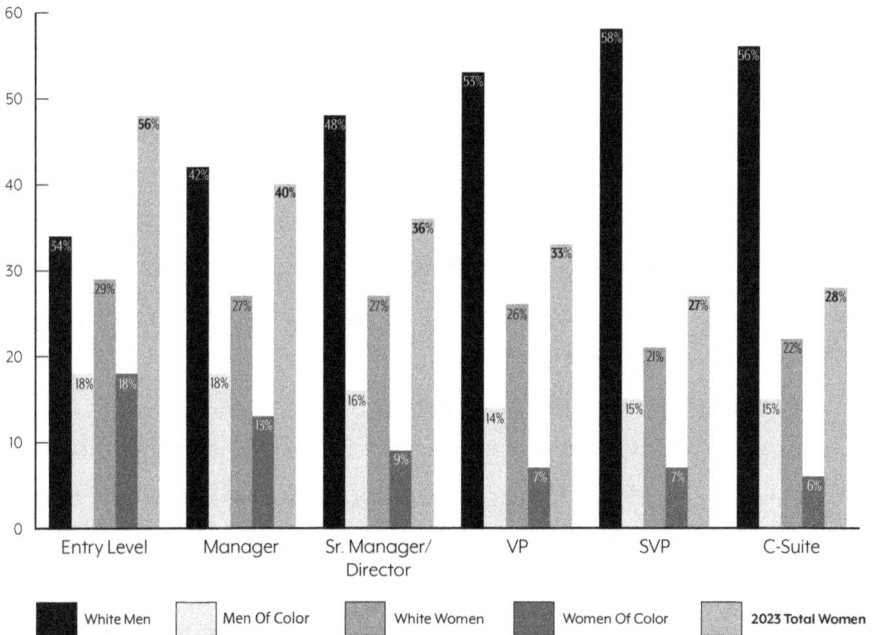

If you are a woman of color or LGBTQIA+ (lesbian, gay, bisexual, transgender, queer questioning, intersex, and/or asexual), it is even worse. The McKinsey study had one woman out of the study at the CEO level who identified as lesbian.

An article focusing on key leadership traits in the *Journal of Personality and Social Psychology* observed traits among men and women leaders. The three key traits were communication (compassion, sensitivity), agency (ambition), and competence (intelligence, creativity).[4]

The Pew Research Center found that women ranked better than or equal to men in eight out of nine leadership traits. Thirty-one percent of the respondents ranked women as more honest than men. Women ranked higher than their male counterparts in compassion and creative leadership traits.[5] A recent analysis, published online in 2019 by *American Psychologist*, shows that most Americans (86%) polled in 2018 think men and women are equally intelligent. However, among those who believe there is a difference, 9% gave the edge to women, compared with only 5% who think men are smarter.[6]

Although women are making progress in leadership, it has been slow going.

Keep reading before you give up in frustration and despair for a lost cause. *Her Rise Her Rules* focuses on your agency and the ways you can energize progress on your career trajectory. It also addresses some of the systemic processes that organizations can modify to increase equity and the number of women in leadership, so you can work on yourself and guide your company from within.

Opportunity is not universal, however.

Currently, women have the majority of caregiving responsibilities. This includes childcare, home care and upkeep, and adult care. Many of us, including myself, care for our aging parents. Due to the exorbitant cost of paid caregiving, many females have made the difficult decision to step out of the workforce or accept reduced pay and responsibility to do caregiving themselves.[7]

A 2024 study by Bieke Biopharmaceuticals found that the average monthly cost to outsource household management in the US is between $4,000 and $5,200.[8]

Women who leave the workforce or step back from a position to take care of responsibilities at home—even for a few years—miss career growth opportunities. They postpone opportunities for advancement, take unpaid leave, and scale back their hours to adjust their lives based on their personal responsibilities.

During the COVID-19 pandemic, a record number of women took on inconsistent work, often without benefits. Many women moved to part-time work, contracting, and freelance jobs to have a more flexible schedule.[9]

Bias Is The Elephant In The Room

Our society and, in turn, our organizations are prone to bias. Each and every one of us has bias. The textbooks we use in schools, the media, and the people we associate with are all influenced by bias. What is most important is to become aware of our biases and try to reframe our mindset.

Awareness gives us power.

Gender bias is a form of unconscious or implicit bias, as well as explicit or conscious bias. It happens when we attribute our attitudes or stereotypes to certain individuals. An example might be a belief that men are less emotional and more analytical. With that bias, if the two final candidates for a finance position are one man and one woman, the male has a stronger chance of being hired for a finance position if those analytical skills are required. This is often the result, even when a female candidate is just as qualified.

Bias is often unconscious but still affects leaders' decisions. It can lead to preferential treatment, unfair assumptions, exclusionary behavior, harassment, or discrimination.

If an organization's culture and leadership do not address this bias, it will lose talented employees and fail to bring ideas and other voices that matter to the table for growth and progress. Organizations could also lose market share due to a lack of insight that serves all those who use its products or services.

Through research and interviews conducted for this book, some key findings arose around negative impacts on women leaders in their mid-level careers. These impacts were based on bias and assumptions grounded in gender stereotypes.

One of the most common assumptions was that women are less committed to their careers as parents than their male peers. The research shows a negative impact on women leaders around hiring, promotion, and pay, which is often termed the "motherhood penalty." Males in the workforce do not experience this same bias, and parenthood was even seen as a positive attribute.[10]

Another bias hindering women's career growth is what is known as the double bind. This is a true either/or form: competence versus likability. A female leader is labeled as a "bitch" if she is more direct, or a mothering figure if she is liked. If a female leader is more kind and nurturing in the work environment, she can be seen as too soft and unable to have hard conversations.

Women leaders typically report the need to clear a higher set of expectational hurdles to be rewarded. This was true for almost every woman leader interviewed for this book.

A hurdle many women leaders face as they rise is that networking opportunities are often highly gendered. Men tend to have greater access to senior male leaders and, therefore, more personal relationships with potential advocates than female leaders.

Critical promotion decisions are made mid-career and are intertwined with the strength of relationships. With men in more of the highest-level positions making the decisions, their relationships with the pipeline of rising leaders are skewed. Often, the people who are promoted are ones where there is a stronger comfort level or the "he is more like me" bias.

Mid-career positions have a strong impact on advancement. We must help senior leadership raise their awareness around bias. Conversations and training with structured transparent criteria around performance can help, and leaders can intentionally provide performance feedback and "feedforward" in an objective, measurable, job-related delivery method and in a timely manner. The feedback should also be actionable and specific for all employees.

Leaders can build a culture that cultivates psychological safety where employees can ask questions and openly discuss bias as a means of problem-solving (not shaming).

Leaders can model appropriate vulnerability, admit when they are wrong, and demonstrate a commitment to learning. It's also about addressing key areas of discrepancies that typically occur with promotions and compensation and increasing transparency.

Each chapter will share "noodling questions" and an application box. The noodling questions are designed to provide an opportunity for introspection on defining what is important to you in your career journey. Below are the questions for this chapter. The application box highlights the major points covered in each chapter.

Three Noodling Questions:

1. Where have you faced bias in your career, and how did you handle it?

2. What did you learn from it, and what might you do differently if it happened today?

3. Where can you lift up or speak up for a female leader?

Application Box ———————————————————

- Currently, women make up only 10.4 percent of the Fortune 500 CEOs.[11] The good news is that we are in a better place than we have been in the past.

- Women of color and those who are LGBTQIA+ have additional hurdles to overcome to be at the highest level of organizations.

- There is a significant opportunity for women in mid-level careers in organizations. Organizations need to be intentional about ensuring women have an equitable way to progress in their careers.

- Bias is prevalent in our organizations, and we all have it. Raising our awareness and implementing training, programs, and processes, as well as ensuring transparency around hiring, promotions, and compensation, are effective ways to overcome it.

2

How To Embrace
What You Can Control

No one else defines you but you.

CHELSEA HANDLER, COMEDIAN AND ACTRESS

I am a lifelong learner, which has served me well throughout my career. In college, I studied political science and English history, and I knew that after college, I would live in Washington, D.C. However, upon my graduation, the political party in power shifted, and the connections I made as a congressional intern in DC were no longer viable.

Neither of these degrees appears frequently on job postings, and I knew I did not want to go to law school. As a young college graduate, I fell into the retail world.

I moved into management with two different major clothing retailers fairly quickly. Until the regional manager level, the vast majority of retail employees were women. At this level and above, almost every leader was white male for women's clothing chains.

After ten years of "retail hell" managing stores, working sixty-to-seventy-hour weeks, and leading thirty-five-plus employees, I knew this was not a sustainable path for me. Although I loved working with people and learned great skills (not least among them superb folding strategies), I did not feel challenged.

After moving back to my home state, I enrolled in a master's program in human relations (MHR) organizational dynamics. While working a few part-time jobs concurrently with the master's program, I also got engaged, married, became pregnant, and moved within seventeen months.

With all the changes and stress, I also acquired my dad's beautiful silver hair but opted to keep it blondish—for now. I was not ready to go full-on silver hair in my thirties. The good news is that my 100-year-old dad still has a great mane of silver hair, so I'll appreciate that someday!

The MHR program required an internship to graduate. I was fortunate to land one with a local energy company in human resources. After learning about the department's potential and what HR does, my reaction was: Wait—is this a job? I could not have found a better fit for my temperament, skills, and potential abilities. It was a true hand-in-glove fit.

The internship led to a full-time job and a significant step in my career journey. I spent twenty-plus years in corporate human resources, leadership development, and top HR roles.

This journey included a few reductions in force for my positions, setbacks that, in hindsight, were catalysts to propel me to the next adventure.

My last role before working for myself was overseeing the development and implementation of a corporate university. Once this was running on full cylinders with the technical training needed, I shared with the firm's CEO what the next development phase would be. This phase was focused on building and strengthening leadership capabilities within the firm.

The CEO told me that neither he nor the board was interested in pursuing this direction. After reflecting on what was key to me, I told the CEO, "Well, you are paying me way too much for what a coordinator could do in this role if that is what you want."

He agreed with me, eliminating my role and bringing in a coordinator. I now know that you should always get severance in writing.

Perhaps not one of my most astute moments—to replace my position before I had another one lined up. That is not the first time, nor will it be the last time, my trusting soul can bite me in the ass. Flourishing in corporate games is not my strong suit.

At the time, it was a punch in the stomach, but it ended up being one of the best things to happen to me. I knew I needed a challenge and growth in any work I undertook. Purpose, making a positive difference, and forward momentum drive me.

I was facing what my current coach, Mark LeBlanc, calls "inspired friction." I just didn't have the words yet to describe that feeling of dread and excitement for forward momentum.

Part of my inspiration called me to work for myself. It just came sooner than I had planned. With two daughters in school and college not too far on the horizon for them, I jumped off the cliff without a parachute.

Let's say it has been quite a roller coaster, with some difficult fiscal quarters and amazing quarters of steady growth. I am lucky to see it all as a learning experience and opportunity for growth.

This year marks my fifteenth year running my own business, and every role, company, community project, and nonprofit board I've served on has contributed to where I am today.

With Heidi Hartman Consulting, I have the honor of working with successful female leaders through coaching, leadership development, team strengthening, and organizational culture development.

Tell me, what is it you plan to do with
your one wild and precious life?
MARY OLIVER, POET

The work is ours. The time is now. We all need to be fully engaged in our purpose so we can solve the issues that matter to us.

Research And Why This Book Now

Through working with amazing clients from both a coaching and consulting standpoint, I observed a difference in career growth between each gender. Over the past fifteen years running Heidi Hartman Consulting and previously in the corporate realm, I have directly experienced hurdles, blocks, and frustrations in my own career trajectory.

The saying "The truth will set you free, but first it will piss you off," has rung true.

Research data about gender inequity in the workplace abounds. Feeling a surge of energy around this topic, I started speaking with women leaders I knew who were achieving great things despite the inequity in organizations and our society.

That led to recommendations from other women leaders I wanted to interview and tap into several female leaders I've coached.

I wanted to ensure I could get a wide range of voices by gathering ideas and concrete actions that women leaders could utilize.

I ended up speaking with over one hundred successful women leaders. They ranged in age from twenty-six to seventy-six. They were in positions and industries ranging from lead principal of an architecture firm to CEO of a zoo, from entrepreneurs to leaders in Fortune 50 organizations, corporate C-suite to manufacturing leaders, executive directors of nonprofits, and everything in between.

I was intentional about curating women's leadership voices from leaders who are women of color and women who identify as LGBTQIA+. Of those I interviewed, just over 30 percent of women leaders were in these groups.

These women leaders shared their time and expertise, relaying stories of epic fails and triumphs throughout their careers. They shared their missteps and how they set their own rules that led to their rise in their organizations. There is much rich information to share from the women I interviewed and the women I've had the honor of coaching.

Through all these conversations, the seven secrets that helped these women rise to the top and set their own career rules emerged.

In this book, Part II outlines seven chapters that reveal the secrets of all those wonderful conversations.

Please find the key topics that speak to you. Take what works for you and might help you leverage your career journey. Find the areas that are best suited to your current journey, focus on them, and make an action plan.

We can only control ourselves, our reaction(s) to challenges or opportunities, and how we want to be intentional about showing up.

We also have *much* more influence and power than we realize.

The powerful women leaders I've had the honor of working with and the amazing women interviewed for this book found ways to follow the rules that worked for them, leading to the rise in their careers. Most of the book is focused on what can be influenced by the individual.

This is not about "fixing" you. You do not need to be fixed.

Each of the seven-secret chapters also includes a story of one of my clients (or a compilation of clients) who faced that particular hurdle. Their names and a few details have been changed to ensure anonymity.

An overview of the seven secrets can help you calibrate which key focus areas are right for you. You are welcome to read them cover to cover or jump into the potential growth area that fits best.

The first secret is about authenticity and becoming the real you: defining and understanding your why or purpose, your true north, and your core values. That journey requires us to become more introspective about how *you* define success, which may differ from what the media or society defines as success. We each bring different strengths and weaknesses to our workplace, and it is imperative to understand and leverage our strengths.

Secret number two focuses on building your support system or curating your "heart hive" to align with your vibe. Our work persona is a brand in the workplace. Is yours portrayed as you would like? Is it authentic? Building a strong network helps you move forward, and the key to that is having the right network. Ensure you are cultivating a strong mix of mentors, advocates, and champions. They are indispensable for your career.

The third secret is getting more comfortable with failure as a stepping stone to success. Curating a growth mindset instead of a fixed one provides you with many more opportunities. Taking smart risks and increasing comfort with exposure to stretch our rubber band is key to moving ahead. Receiving clear and specific feedback is how we grow.

The fourth secret will help you find your voice and ensure it is heard, finding your inner lion and letting her roar. We gain strength by driving to action despite the fear we may feel and coming from a place of curiosity. Conflict is not evil but a natural part of seeing things through different lenses. Setting goals that are meaningful for you and align with the organization's top priorities is key to success.

Secret five will help you elevate your "IQ" or "*influence* quotient" as your superpower. As a leader, work gets done through influence. When working with others, start where they are, and be transparent and clear in communication while you harness the power of storytelling. To be successful, focus on the benefits of engagement or what's in it for them—WIIFT.

The sixth secret outlines the number one differentiator for women leaders in the workplace: visibility. Many women leaders tend to concentrate on the "heads-down" mode of knocking work out of the park, "If I do a great job on this report/project/communication, then I will get noticed." Research shows that, in fact, visibility in all key interactions is what moves female leaders to higher ranks.[12] Curating ways to build your work brand, enlisting advocates, and navigating visibility with higher levels of leadership significantly affect your work growth for the positive.

Moving from surviving to thriving is the seventh secret. When it comes to emotional intelligence (EI), the head and the heart are intertwined. Emotions are not good or bad and can be both helpful and harmful in the workplace. It's about how we manage our emotions and increase our awareness. Know how to show up for higher-stakes conversations and connect with others intentionally. One great tool that can help is understanding your modus operandi (MO or preferences) in how you show up and share that information with others you work with.

The seven secrets of successful women leaders encompass traits and tactics that give us direct influence within our workplace. All seven may not apply in your current season. Take what works for you and leave the rest, focusing on what you can control and influence.

Several other systemic and societal obstacles prevent women leaders from rising. Organizations that want to attract and advance key talent can address those obstacles. Part III of the book outlines many of those opportunities and recommends ideas to improve organizational systems.

?-?-?-

Three Noodling Questions:

1. When thinking about your career trajectory, which of the seven-secrets chapters might benefit you most?

2. Who is a powerful female leader you admire who has achieved great things in her career, and what specifically do you admire?

3. What challenges in your career have made you a stronger leader and helped you grow?

Application Box ─────────────────────────

- Understand and appreciate the journey your career has taken so far.

- Based on the seven-secrets chapters, choose one you want to take a deeper dive into exploring.

- Define ways to embrace what you can control and commit to how you want to move forward.

PART II

The Seven Secrets Of Successful Leaders

3

The Real You—
The State Of Becoming
(Secret 1)

The final forming of a person's character lies in their own hands.

ANNE FRANK, DIARIST

Y ou are the architect of your life and career. It's up to you to define and increase the odds of your success and how much you thrive. If we fail to determine what is important to us, our values, our why, and what success means, and we fail to understand our strengths and work style, others will define it for us.

The quote attributed to psychologist Carl Jung is especially true for women leaders: "The world will ask you who you are, and if you don't know, the world will tell you."

People love to provide advice and will "should" all over you.

Well-meaning folks "should-ed" all over me when I started my firm in 2010. At the time, I didn't realize the importance of tuning into the right fit for me.

Some of the "should-ing" I received included the following:

- "You should do human resources for small companies."
- "You should go back and get your PhD."
- "You should only work in the energy sector."
- "You should go back to work for a company that has benefits."
- "You should write a book before you start a business so you're an 'expert.'"
- "You should take a year off and get every certification that will validate you for the work you want to do."

The truth is that none of those suggestions supported the "why" or purpose that was important to me and gave me energy. We each must carve the path that is best for us.

Remember, it is not selfish to do what is best for you. In fact, you'll bring the best of yourself to improve lives around you.

Be prepared to spot growth opportunities when they present themselves—because they are the key learning opportunities. You'll know because they make you uncomfortable, and your initial impulse may be that you're not ready. But remember: Growth and comfort never co-exist.
GINNI ROMETTY, FORMER CHAIR, PRESIDENT, AND CEO OF IBM

Robin's Story Of Becoming

Robin (like all stories in the book, this story is true, but the name[s] have been changed) is a marketing maven and communications leader in Texas. We first connected through some team development I facilitated, and she later reached out for coaching.

Robin had always been clear about the value she brought to the organization. Her organization was going through an acquisition, and things were shifting for her professionally and personally.

She felt she was trying to build a new leadership team and department on sand without a solid base. Everything was shifting. Although she was comfortable with ambiguity, Robin felt this situation was different for her.

As we unpacked her experiences, she found her way back to her true voice. During our time together, Robin tapped into several tools and exercises I provided. She could zero in on purpose and how it aligned with her work.

Robin also revisited and revised the core values that spoke to her essence. After much soul-searching, she realized that her values were not aligned with her organization's core values.

After nine years with this organization, Robin discovered that her definition of success had changed. What was once so vital to her was replaced by a different definition of success. She wanted independence, flexibility, and to make a difference.

After investing time, work, and money in herself, Robin came to the decision that it was time to move on to a new adventure. The work she wanted to do and the clients she wanted to work with were no longer aligned with her current career track.

The good news is that Robin's organization was generous in investing in developing its employees. She and I went through several assessments that highlighted her strengths and opportunities. Robin had strong self-awareness and awareness of others and was adept at meeting people where they were.

Robin decided to bet on herself and started her own firm. She has grown her firm significantly over the last few years. Robin has built a strong employee base by leveraging many of the tools we utilized and by investing in her employees.

Know Your Purpose And Your Why

As long as you're operating from a place of stress,
you won't be able to operate from a place of purpose.
BETSY ALLEN-MANNING, SPEAKER AND AUTHOR

We are told to find our passion—and if you live it, you will never work a day in your life.

From personal experience, and that of so many women I've spoken to, that's a bunch of BS.

Instead, reframe that intimidating suggestion and think through the lens that passion is the *how*, not the *what*. It's the way you feel and what brings you energy, what fills you up, and how you live.

The task of finding your passion seems daunting and maybe even overwhelming. It needn't be. Each of us has a unique voice and a purpose inside that provides direction.

A quote often attributed to Mark Twain that fuels the work I get to do: "The two most important days in your life are the day you are born and the day you find out why."

I have this quote above my desk. It is so meaningful to me because in my work with women leaders, I get to help them on their journey to find their calling or why.

One of my clients, Katie, knew by age five that she wanted to be an architect and run a firm. Most of us are not that lucky, and we kiss a few frogs before finding our gifts. Another friend of mine chose her first college major as Speech Pathology. She may be the most impatient person I know, and she bolted to her advisor's office to change her major after seeing the students spend the entire class period learning to teach a client to say the "t" sound.

Luckily for us, there are some great assessments and exercises we can take to aid our journey to finding our true north.

Look for clues about things that fuel your energy and those that deplete you. Make a list of each. Your energy is currency. Spend it well. Invest in it wisely.

Capture stories that have been meaningful in your life and helped shape you. Find common threads between them. Write down what fueled your passion, either good or bad.

Partner with someone who is open and has a reputation for being curious and good at asking questions. Share some key stories that helped shape you, and learn what threads and commonalities they see in you.

Each of these can help you define your purpose and can direct you to options that give you energy and fill your bucket. We can find fun and passion in our work.

Each of us has a core or essence that defines us based on key positive and negative experiences. These key experiences can point us in the direction of our purpose.

One day, when I was in middle school, my mom shared that I would not attend school that day. After I jumped for joy, she told me we were heading to the state capitol to join a march, and we were fighting for equal rights for women. I can still tap into the positive energy of that day, surrounded by a community fighting for the rights of others.

It was one of the many experiences that directed me to my purpose.

We are often tired and imbalanced not because
we are doing too much but because
we are doing too little of what is most real and meaningful.
MARIANNE WILLIAMSON, AUTHOR AND POLITICIAN

Core Values And True North

Most organizations have a list of values that guide their work and state what they stand for. As individuals, we each have a set of values that guide our behavior and how we interact with others.

It is important to define the set of values you want to live within and what living those values looks and does not look like.

Move your core values from inspirational to ingraining them in everything you do, including your decisions.

When our values do not align with those of the organization we work for, we experience incongruity and friction. There is also friction when we do not act in accordance with our own core values.

Try to focus on your primary core values, between three to no more than seven. Any more than seven, and you won't remember them.

The list of potential core values below combines about three lists I've used with my clients. At the end, there are some spaces for you to add values that are important to you should the right fit not appear on this list.

First, circle all that apply and jump out to you. After that, narrow that list to a top ten list. Once you have a top ten list, whittle that down to your three-to-seven range. Keep working until there is a number that is most meaningful to your core or your essence. Remember, not more than seven.

Core Values List

Accountability
Achievement
Adaptability
Adventure
Altruism
Ambition
Authenticity
Balance
Belonging
Caring
Collaboration
Commitment
Community
Compassion
Competence
Competition
Confidence
Connection
Contribution
Cooperation
Courage
Creativity
Curiosity
Dignity
Diversity
Efficiency
Environment
Equality
Ethics
Excellence
Fairness
Faith
Family
Financial freedom
Flexibility
Forgiveness
Freedom
Friendship

Frugality
Fun
Generosity
Giving back
Grace
Gratitude
Growth
Harmony
Health
Honesty
Hope
Humility
Humor
Inclusion
Independence
Initiative
Integrity
Job security
Joy
Justice
Kindness
Knowledge
Leadership
Learning
Legacy
Leisure
Love
Loyalty
Making a difference
Nature
Openness
Optimism
Order
Parenting
Patience
Peace
Perseverance
Personal fulfillment

Power
Pride
Recognition
Reliability
Resourcefulness
Respect
Responsibility
Risk-taking
Safety
Security
Self-discipline
Self-expression
Self-respect
Service
Simplicity
Spirituality
Sportsmanship
Stewardship
Success
Teamwork
Time
Tradition
Travel
Trust
Truth
Understanding
Uniqueness
Usefulness
Vision
Vulnerability
Wealth
Well-being
Wholeheartedness
Wisdom
Other:

_____

_____

_____

Defining Success

Society bombards us with images of what success should look like. Advertisers display their definitions of "pretty," "rich," or "successful." Social media paints pictures, highlights filtered photographs, and shares stories about the perfect life, displaying the lives of people who seem perfect and have it all.

First, please understand that no one is as perfect as they seem to be. We all have flaws and face-plants. Stop the doom-scrolling and curate your information intake and feeds.

Do not judge or compare your current circumstances to someone's highlight reel.

Next, it's time to (as my dad, Tex Hartman, says) "contemplate the lint in your belly button."

Look inward and consider what success means to you. What is truly important? Tune into your unique voice. Review the values you have claimed for your list.

Some of my friends and colleagues define success as power, recognition, and money. For others, it is travel, kindness, giving back, and harmony. For me, it's curiosity, collaboration, inclusion, equity, and authenticity. The only "right" answer is the one that resonates for you.

Success is living your values on your terms in a way that is right for you.

From a professional perspective, I feel successful when I work with clients I enjoy and when they live lives aligned with their definition of success and their core values.

I want those I love to know in their heart that I love them and that there is joy in my life. It is not important to me to have a fancy car, or a crap ton of money. I do desire enough money to pay bills, buy fun art, and go on travel adventures with extra to donate to the causes that speak to my heart.

You need to define what is important to you to be successful. This definition may change as you reach different milestones or seasons in your life. It is important, however, that it continues to align with your core values.

Strengths And Workplace Style

I can do things you cannot, you can do things I cannot;
together we can do great things.
MOTHER TERESA, NUN AND MISSIONARY

Every individual has gifts and opportunities. Often, our strengths and opportunities are two sides of the same coin.

Our lives and our careers are not about trying to shore up the areas where we are not as strong. They are about leveraging those traits where we excel and tapping into folks who can bring strengths we don't possess.

Sometimes, it is hard to know our strengths because they come so easily to us. We might find ourselves coveting someone else's strengths because they are not a gift we possess.

A strength that I possess is articulating a vision and seeing connections.

A huge weakness or opportunity for me is the details. For projects requiring detail, I partner up with someone with strong process and attention-to-detail capabilities. We are better together, like chocolate and peanut butter.

When clients are stuck on defining their strengths, one of the exercises we use is to have them send out an email to a minimum of twenty to twenty-five acquaintances. We ask them to, if possible, send an email to close to an equal number of acquaintances in each of the following categories—but to try to send more work-related emails:

- Work colleagues
- Clients
- Family
- Friends
- Volunteering colleagues

Send the emails individually—or blind copy (bcc) so folks don't think, "Oh, I don't need to answer if they sent it to twenty people."

The body of the email should read as follows:

> *Hello, I have a favor to ask you.*
>
> *I'm completing an exercise that seeks to pinpoint my unique abilities/key strengths.*
>
> *I'm looking for feedback from you. I value your opinion and ask the following question and request you get back to me within forty-eight hours:*
>
> *What do you see as my key strengths/unique abilities?*
>
> *These might include my talents and abilities, characteristics that describe me, how I do things that produce positive results, what I'm good at and passionate about, what you can count on me for, and any other distinguishing characteristics.*
>
> *As a bonus, please share what you believe to be my superpower.*
>
> *I appreciate your time and effort.*

Once the responses arrive, patterns and groupings will emerge, clarifying your strengths and gifts. Consider the patterns and what gives you energy and what you enjoy. What might be ways to leverage those strengths?

Many tools and assessments provide clarity around your workplace and communication style. At the top of my list is an assessment tool I utilize in most engagements: Insights Discovery, developed in Dundee, Scotland. Insights Discovery has this wonderful "simplexity" (easy to understand, lots of research validity behind the assessment) to the tool. After answering twenty-five questions, you receive a report providing deep insight into how you are wired and how to use it to your advantage.[13]

Awareness of our values, our why or purpose, and our strengths is difficult and rewarding work. As far as we know, we have one life to live on this planet—and if we don't live it with intention, defining what is important and successful for us, we miss our opportunity.

Three Noodling Questions:

1. What are your core values (no more than seven) and your true north (purpose or why)?

2. What does success look like to you?

3. What are the strengths you bring to the workplace?

Application Box

- Invest in yourself. Get a coach to help you navigate where you are, what is next for you, or what is possible.

- Invest time and brain power in defining your purpose, core values, what success looks like for you, and your strengths and opportunities.

- Do the work so you understand what is unique to you and find a place that honors your voice.

4

Curate Your Heart Hive To Align With Your Vibe
(Secret 2)

Surround yourself with only people who are going to lift you higher.
OPRAH WINFREY, TALK SHOW HOST AND AUTHOR

Think about the circle of people who surround you. I call this circle your heart hive. The people you hang around with either lift you up or they suck happiness out of your life. Choose wisely.

It's crucial to curate the individuals in your inner circle. Build a hive of supporters who are committed to helping you grow and thrive. This is a fundamental aspect of your personal and professional journey.

Your hive is both a sanctuary and a catalyst. It should be as dynamic, resilient, and bright as you aspire to be. Choose your hive wisely. Ensure you nurture your personal and professional brand and build substantial relationships.

Remember, you are the architect of your success, positioning yourself to thrive and shine.

The crew you choose needs to be one of mutual growth, support, and celebration. You want a small group comprising your inner circle.

You will also want a team of mentors, champions, advocates, and a strong network.

These are the people who will be there for you, supporting your professional growth and celebrating your successes.

This team should help you overcome obstacles. Design a hive of people you can bounce ideas off, who can lift you up when needed, and who will call you out when necessary. Within this hive, you support each other and act as connectors for development.

As part of your journey to and within leadership, think about your brand, who you spend time with, and the growth of your network. Developing and maintaining a robust team of mentors, champions, and advocates is also imperative. You may need to prune a few of the people who don't belong in your heart hive anymore. Just like pruning a tree can help it grow stronger, letting some people go may improve your growth as well.

Find a group of people who challenge and inspire you.
Spend a lot of time with them, and it will change your life.
AMY POEHLER, ACTOR AND COMEDIAN

Isabel's Hive Mirroring Vibe Story

Isabel is a force for good. She owns an accounting and audit firm that specializes in the nonprofit space. Most of Isabel's clients came through referrals, but she did not have the volume of work she wanted.

Unfortunately, Isabel and her firm were the best-kept secret of some of the nonprofits in her city.

After working on her success story and truly defining her best-fit client, she was ready for the next step. She asked a cross-section of people to share their definitions of her brand.

We worked on understanding her current brand versus the brand she wanted. Once Isabel knew the gap between what her clients and others in the community thought and what she wanted as a brand, she could address it.

Isabel then defined her success story by who she was and precisely how she helped her clients. She was also clear on her best-fit clients and claimed the brand identity she wanted. Since these were aligned, Isabel could articulate her success story to her current clients and others in the community and how they could help her help others through the great work she did in her firm.

Isabel had a fairly strong network within the community. One area she had not previously leveraged was involvement in a nonprofit professional organization where she could connect with regional executive directors.

Once she joined the nonprofit professional organization, Isabel developed stronger relationships with several key executive directors. She lifted her visibility and connected with her ideal clients.

She also had a solid heart hive of other women leaders whom she could confide in—except for one person. One of the folks within Isabel's circle was what she experienced as a taker.

There are givers and takers in this world. Author Adam Grant provides more context in his book *Give and Take: Why Helping Others Drives Our Success.*

Givers ask, "What can I do for you?" They have others' best interests at heart. This doesn't mean they also don't have their own interest at heart.

Takers focus on service for themselves. They tend to ask, "What can you do for me?" Although takers may rise quickly in an organization, they typically don't stay at the top.[14]

The key to being a healthy giver is ensuring some key criteria are in place. You must get clear on your boundaries to protect yourself from burnout. Within organizations, we want to create a culture that is open to asking for help and where takers do not thrive.

This woman was consistently asking Isabel for favors without reciprocation or appreciation. We worked through how to distance herself from this coworker and put some boundaries in place. It took a while, but Isabel can now utilize the formerly depleted energy in more positive ways.

The one area Isabel needed to be stronger in was having good mentors, advocates, and champions. An effective tool I've used with several clients is an influence map. This map identifies the key stakeholders and where they may stand as an ally, neutral party, or someone who may potentially work against you.

We completed an influence map of the stakeholders, influencers, and critical people Isabel needed to know. Then, Isabel ranked them and assessed her current relationship with them using a red/yellow/green system.

She is now working on bridging those relationships that will help her grow—green, of course.

Since Isabel is a giver, it is easy for her to ensure the relationships she is growing are reciprocal. She provides value to those she has as her mentors, advocates, and champions.

Isabel has also grown more comfortable with setting boundaries to curtail the takers' pull on her resources.

Isabel's firm and support system have grown significantly. Most importantly, she works with clients she enjoys and provides services so her clients can better serve the community.

You As A Brand

Everyone has brands they are fond of or loyal to. One of mine is Jif peanut butter (either crunchy or creamy). Think about some of your favorite brands. What is it about them that earns your loyalty? What drives your strong preference?

One of my clients moves a lot for her job and is a raving fan of Starbucks. She knows she is settled in when her corner Starbucks knows her name and beverage of choice, at least until her next move.

Just like Jif peanut butter, people have brands. When others meet you, they gauge your energy, how you carry yourself, and how you interact with people.

Your brand is also your social media presence, communication style, and the way you speak and lead, which are all part of who you project. Your story and how you present yourself builds influence through your behaviors, qualities, and skills. It is what you are known for.

How would others define your brand? How would you define your brand? Is it communicating the leader you would like to project? Does it embody your values and the type of leader you would like to be? Does it project the authentic you?

Make sure you validate your beliefs regarding your brand. One way is to do an internet search on yourself and view your social media presence with a more removed eye. Another great way to do this is to check the alignment between what you desire to project and what others see with this simple exercise.

Ask twenty to twenty-five people who have experienced and know you to define your brand. Do the same exercise as I did for Isabel. You want authenticity, unity, and consistency in how you come across and how others see you.

If this is not the case, what is the gap, and what is one thing you can shift that will give you the most traction to your desired brand? You want to ensure that your brand is an authentic reflection of yourself.

Your brand should paint a picture of your success. Your success story shows your possibility and potential for the next level. It is focused on future value and tied to the organizational goals.

Own your success. Your accomplishments are a testament to your capabilities and resilience.

Network Is Not A Dirty Word

Relationships are powerful. Creating connections based on shared goals and interests helps you in your job. People are drawn to and want to work with those they like, respect, and trust.

If you would rather take a fork to your eye than network, reframe networking as an opportunity to meet others and share experiences. Networking is a chance to help others and let them advocate for you and help you be more successful. Looking for ways to provide value for others is a great way to get more comfortable with the practice of networking.

When you prioritize building relationships, you become more successful. Decide what your priorities are, what your values are, and what is important to you. Look at your schedule to see if your calendar reflects what is important to you. If you want to grow in your career, you must invest in the right relationships.

Networking is more than a one-and-done or a way to climb in your career. It is about building meaningful, enduring relationships. Nurture these connections not only to survive but to thrive. Relationships create partnerships where both parties receive value. It is an investment that needs to be tended to.

You also want to amplify other women. When you authentically shine a light on others, the light will reflect back on you. When we help someone else rise, we all shine.

Some women in leadership have a scarcity mindset. They may feel threatened by other women leaders and sabotage or put others down to appear better. I don't see this behavior as often as I did earlier in my career, thankfully, but occasionally, an insecure "it-will-only-be-me" climber will show up. Limit your exposure to these people.

There is plenty of room for us all to succeed in leadership. As former US Secretary of State Madeleine Albright said, "There's a special place in hell for women who don't help other women."

Building relationships and networking is an art. Seek out people you admire and ask them to share their journey stories.

The best ways to grow your network are to be curious, ask questions, and listen. You should also find methods to follow up with your network and provide value to them. Focus on helping others become successful. Deposit into the relationship account before making withdrawals. Find your spirit of generosity.

Some tips or ideas to grow your networking savvy are the following:

- Come from a place of curiosity and ask questions.
- Be open and approachable.
- Connect people with others you think they should know or who might help them.
- Provide value to others. (Share resources, articles, quotes, or book recommendations that might be helpful or made you think of them.)
- Connect with a friend to let them know you are thinking about them (phone, email, text, handwritten note).
- Nominate someone you believe deserves an award.
- Send someone you know a book that inspired you.
- Find a cause that speaks to your heart, volunteer, and connect with other leaders who care about the same cause.

Mentors, Advocates, And Champions, Oh My!

Each one of us is born with a box of matches inside us,
but we can't strike them all by ourselves.
LAURA ESQUIVEL, AUTHOR

Mentors offer wisdom and support and help you learn.

Advocates voice your capabilities.

Champions or sponsors fight for your progression and say your name in rooms where you are not *yet* invited. They create opportunities for you. Typically, they choose you.

Grow and nurture mentors, advocates, and champions both within and outside your organization. Know what skills are essential in your business and for your next leap.

As you navigate your professional landscape, moving ahead requires allies, mentors, advocates, and champions. You should have several of these. Your network should include people within your organization, as well as in the community or other organizations.

You may ask, "How do I get a sponsor?" Your professional narrative is pivotal. Be authentic and conversational in the way you tell your success story. Excel in your work, making your accomplishments known authentically. You should also be an ally to others and lift them up.

Show the results and the impact of your work. Start at the macro level; align yourself with the business objectives. Where there are gaps, make sure you do the work to close them.

Venture outside of your job and department as well as your professional arena. Build relationships in different contexts.

Join a board that speaks to your heart. Think about connecting with folks who have similar hobbies. People with outside perspectives enrich your professional narrative. They bring a touch of diversity and vibrancy.

The Five Folks You Spend The Most Time With

Who do you spend most of your time with outside of your family? Research shows we are influenced by those with whom we spend the greatest amount of time.

Our close relationships influence our lives, behaviors, and habits. They can affect our way of thinking, values, self-esteem, goals, and decisions.

Think about the list of your closest relationships, and if they have the influence you would like them to. Are these relationships building you up, or sucking you dry?

All our relationships have seasons. Some friendships serve us, and sometimes we have friendships that no longer serve us. Is it time to sunset a friendship or distance yourself?

As Queen Beyoncé aptly puts it, "The world will see you the way you see you and treat you the way you treat yourself."

Curate your heart hive because it reflects your vibe. Nurture it, and you will go far.

Three Noodling Questions

1. How can you cultivate the right mentors, champions, and advocates? What connections do you need to make, and what can you do to help them?

2. Is your desired brand the one you have now? If so, great! If not, how do you need to show up that is more authentically you?

3. What intentionality do you need to bring to building a more robust network that serves your goals?

Application Box

- Define your brand. Ask twenty to twenty-five people who have worked with you and some who know you well to define your brand. You want authenticity, unity, and consistency in how you come across and how others see you. You want alignment between what you *want* to project and what you are actually projecting.

- Prioritize building relationships. If you want to grow in your career, you must invest in the right relationships and build the right network. Nurture these connections to not only survive but to thrive.

- Work toward making yourself worthy of having a champion or sponsor. Know what resources you need to support yourself and your work. Have a short story highlighting your accomplishments that your champion can easily share.

- Have confidence in yourself. If you don't believe in yourself, others won't believe in you. Maintain a list of your wins and achievements, what I call a sunshine folder.

5

The *F* Word—
Failing Can Equal Success
(Secret 3)

Raise your hand, take risks, and don't fear failure—
it's one of the biggest impediments to success.
CATHY ENGELBERT, CEO OF DELOITTE

Face-plants are part of our journey to success. If we put ourselves out there, we will fail. If we don't put ourselves out there and take chances, we will not succeed. We need to ensure we see failure as a stepping stone on our journey to success.

Remember, your ancestors outnumber your fears. Step into your power.

Discomfort is the currency to your success.
BROOKE CASTILLO, COACH

Cultivating a growth mindset and expanding our horizons are key to reaching senior leadership. By becoming more comfortable with risk, we experience new things, learn, and grow.

Feedback can redirect us to an improved approach, point to a new way of viewing things, and help us understand how we come across to others.

I was head of human resources for an architecture and engineering firm during my midcareer. One of the things I implemented was notification of transitions for our employees, not only recognizing folks for coming on board or leaving but also for those obtaining degrees or certifications, doing volunteer board service, etc.

For this story, it's important to know that I lived in a small West Texas town in my formative years, where I did not receive a great English grammar base, and on top of that, I am a bit "lexdystic" (dyslexic) and cannot spell worth a damn. These are the reasons my spell-check is always on.

I had just sent a company-wide email welcoming back Sasha, an old familiar face joining the sports architecture team. It was a lovely email about how excited we were that Sasha returned and how much we appreciated her.

Within five seconds of the email going out, I had three people at my door: "Heidi, did you intend to send that out?" Well, of course I did; I'm looking forward to working with Sasha again.

They then pointed out that I had sent this company-wide email out that actually said:

"Please join me in welcoming back an old *failure* face, Sasha, joining the sports architecture team." Spell-check changed my word from *familiar* to *failure* and I did not catch it.

After a few swear words and a beet-red face, I flew past them and up the stairs to speak with Sasha and apologize profusely. Let's just say she was more gracious than I deserved.

Then, I sent an apology email to the entire company, correcting and owning my mistake. It was a highlight of an area of growth for me as I try my best to cultivate a growth mindset.

Some of the tools to utilize and shift our perception of failure include seeing opportunities instead of obstacles by adopting a growth mindset, expanding our horizons, getting more comfortable with risk, and being open to constructive and positive feedback.

There is no such thing as failure.
Failure is just life trying to move us in another direction.
OPRAH WINFREY, TALK SHOW HOST AND AUTHOR

Paula's Failure-To-Success Story

Paula was in line for the head of the technology department at her company. Her boss shared that she was "the succession plan" for his job.

She was in an organization that had become increasingly toxic leading up to an acquisition. The company was becoming more political, with much posturing from her peers. Her boss was given a severance package and quickly left the organization.

Paula enjoyed working with the fantastic clients they supported but no longer felt connected to her organization's culture.

There had been many changes, but she perceived them as negative and adopted a fixed mindset. With her biggest supporter's exit, Paula was unsure where she stood.

As fate would have it, a hotshot "golden boy" in the company being acquired was offered the role that Paula thought was in the bag for her.

When she and I met, her confidence was low; she felt blindsided because her past feedback had been so positive. She was ready for a change. Paula did have a few internal leaders she trusted, and we worked on a script to approach each of them to get a clearer picture of what happened.

Through some 360-degree feedback, her meeting with the two leaders, and some self-reflection, Paula found she had not been receiving clear and specific feedback, which had derailed her.

Senior leadership did not see that Paula had the confidence, optimism, and growth mindset to wield the influence required for the chief technology officer role. They also believed Paula played it too safe and didn't have the risk agility they needed for the position. Paula did have many of those attributes but the senior leadership was not aware of that fact.

Through our work together, Paula shifted to a growth mindset, identified and seized opportunities, made educated decisions, and stretched her risk agility. Paula also completed an influence map of key stakeholders and their hidden agendas so she could leverage her influence.

One of Paula's vendors took notice of the changes she saw in Paula and knew she was the perfect fit for their chief technology officer opening.

Paula joined the new organization after several conversations about culture and clarity in expectations on both sides. As part of her onboarding, she also negotiated to have a coach for her first year to set her up for success.

Growth Versus Fixed Mindset And Expanding Horizons

You gain strength, courage, and confidence by every experience
in which you really stop to look fear in the face . . .
Do the thing you think you cannot do.
ELEANOR ROOSEVELT, FIRST LADY AND DIPLOMAT

Carol S. Dweck is a psychologist, researcher, and the author of *Mindset*. Her key premise is that how you think determines your life's course as early as your preschool years.

You learn one of two mindsets growing up. One is that personal qualities like intelligence and the ability to change are unchangeable and innate, known as a fixed mindset. The second is that you believe you can change and grow your intelligence and ability, or a growth mindset.[15]

Brain research shows that when you adopt or have learned a fixed mindset, it shrinks your ability to access options. The opposite is true if you train your brain to adopt a growth mindset. With a growth mindset, your options expand, as does your ability to be more solutions-centric. You expand your horizons with new possibilities.[16]

Once you understand this, you can intentionally adjust your mindset to be more growth-focused. Your mindset influences careers, relationships, the way you parent, and overall life satisfaction.

I'm not afraid of storms, for I'm learning how to sail my ship.
LOUISA MAY ALCOTT, AUTHOR

Risk—Getting Comfortable Being Uncomfortable

Decide whether or not the goal is worth the risks involved.
If it is, stop worrying.
AMELIA EARHART, AVIATION PIONEER

Whether you are in the curiosity-killed-the-cat or the hold-my-beer category of risk, comfort determines your career growth. There is no innovation without risk; taking smart risks is essential to climbing the leadership ladder.

Women are perceived as being more risk-averse than males in the workplace. Much of this perception comes from people's biases in defining risk. Many women are grouped in the stereotype of being perfectionists or collaborators. With these labels, people assume that women leaders are not comfortable with taking risks. We must work to debunk stereotypes that portray most women as perfectionists or collaborators.

You have influence over how you're perceived by others, especially concerning smart risks. Leaders make decisions based on research, experience, and the information available to them while assessing risk. Learning to take *educated* risks, which can be uncomfortable at first, is vital if you want to reach a leadership position.

One key is to increase your comfort with risk. Our minds make us believe failure will be worse than it is. As humans, we are hardwired to avoid uncertainty. But it is rare that we will realize the worst-case scenario. The way to increase your comfort or tolerance is to take risks. Start by taking smaller risks, and you will build up to larger risks.

When you mix up your routine(s) and try new things, you can increase your comfort with change. Another way to increase your comfort is to surround yourself with people who are risk-takers.

There is risk in everything we do, including *not* taking the risk. Get curious about your discomfort with risk; instead of perceiving it as a stop sign, see it as inviting a choice. Think about the probability that the odds are in your favor and that the gain will offset the loss.

Change and risk can cause anxiety. When you reframe anxiety as excitement, it reduces your aversion to risk. Research shows that anxiety and excitement are physiologically identical.

Taking calculated risks is a powerful way to advance in your career. Concentrating on calculated risk(s) helps you understand what risks are worth taking and why. Not making a move is risky and can rob you of opportunities and growth.

When you clearly define your values and goals personally and professionally, risk helps clarify what is important. That helps you maintain forward momentum through the decision-making process.

Risk-takers are catalysts, operating in offense mode. When facts are blended with imagination, innovation and new solutions result.

Balance the facts you know, potential consequences, organizational values, defined goals, and what potential path(s) will get you to your goal. Try to give yourself many possibilities for success and build your tolerance for ambiguity. Also, know that you will only win sometimes and when to be comfortable with good enough.

The Other *F* Word—*Feedback*

They say don't listen to negativity and surround yourself with positivity. I say, "Be strong enough to hear it, accept what is true, improve yourself, and throw the rest in the trash."

RACHEL MATHEW, AUTHOR

Feedback is critical to your success. Unfortunately, in the workplace, women rarely receive the feedback they need. Their male counterparts receive feedback on the substance of their work, whereas women typically receive feedback on their personality. Even when women ask for actionable, constructive feedback, it's often not as specific or on the substance of their work.[17]

Women are almost one and a half times more likely to receive subjective negative feedback than objective and constructive feedback compared to their male counterparts. Male counterparts are typically provided clarity around their strengths with specificity on where they can improve.[18]

This imbalance impairs women's advancement into senior leadership roles.

Research published in the *Harvard Business Review* shows four significant differences in feedback between men and women: vision, political skills, asserting leadership, and confidence. These differences can push employees toward different career paths. In addition to identifying these differences, the article provides potential strategies for addressing them.[19]

Regarding vision, women tend to receive feedback about their delivery versus the development of the vision. To remedy this, building on suggestions the *Harvard Business Review* article made for managers, women employees can ask for specific input on the development of the vision. Some clarification you can share includes your personal vision for the team you lead or the organization. You also want to share how that vision fits within the bigger picture. Get feedback on what areas of expertise you need to develop to advance to the next leadership level.

Women also tend to hear different feedback about their political skills. Political skills include behaviors like negotiating, influencing, and networking, which are crucial to senior leadership roles. Many women tend to avoid politics in the workplace, perhaps envisioning a smarmy used-car salesman with a lousy comb-over who wears too much cheap aftershave.

Try to enthusiastically adopt a political perspective and see it as strengthening your influence to achieve your individual and organizational goals. Complete an influence map of key stakeholders to uncover potential hidden agendas. Forge strong working relationships with those in power.

Regarding feedback about asserting leadership, most women are encouraged to get along with others. In contrast, men are typically told to be assertive and pursue more leadership roles. To counter this, share your leadership aspirations and development goals, asking who can help you.

Confidence is the final feedback area identified with significant gender differences. Men are told to develop confidence in particular skills, while in contrast, women tend to receive more generalized feedback about being more self-confident without specific instructions on how to do that.

To circumvent this, ask for specific feedback on key skill sets involving confidence, how to leverage them within your role, and how to better display your confidence.

Sometimes, you must help your leader deliver the feedback you need to hear by asking questions and sharing your strengths and areas of development. When your goal is the senior leadership level(s), develop a growth mindset to help expand your horizons. You will also want to strengthen your agility around taking smart risks.

Ensure that you receive the developmental feedback you need to leverage your strengths and mitigate any potential derailments that could hinder your path to success.

Three Noodling Questions

1. What can you learn from a past failure?

2. How can you give yourself more grace when you have a screwup?

3. How do you shift your mindset to adopt a growth mindset and be more open to feedback?

Application Box ─────────────────────────

- Foster a growth mindset that opens more possibilities and expands your horizons.

- Develop your risk agility. Assess risk from emotional and data-driven perspectives; take small risks that grow your muscle and comfort level, eventually taking on larger, educated risks. Surround yourself with champions of smart risk.

- Help your leader provide specific, clear, and actionable feedback outlining the need to grow your knowledge, skills, and abilities.

- Build feedback from other trusted sources, such as peers, mentors, and advocates.

6

Find Your Inner Lion
(Secret 4)

Use. Your. Voice. No one is just like you. You have a unique voice, and it needs to be heard. Find your inner lion and speak up. Channel any fear you may have and think of it as an opportunity. We grow most in places of discomfort. We need courage to move forward when we feel fear.

Some key factors in finding your inner lion include using your voice to drive action, overcoming and embracing the suck of conflict and boundaries, finding ways to leverage your curiosity, and defining and setting goals with tenacity.

Female staffers in the Obama administration developed the "amplification" strategy to make women heard. Under that method, women leaders repeat and give credit when another woman leader shares a good idea.[20] We can lift and support each other in the workplace.

Ideas to amplify women's voices include the following:

- Offer to be a spokesperson or presenter
- Email the group, spelling out people's roles/responsibilities
- Keep track of accomplishments in real time
- Create a file for the specific purpose of tracking concrete accomplishments

In her book *How Women Decide*, Therese Huston suggests that gender bias is a pervasive problem in who speaks up and who receives credit.[21] Our society has instilled gender-norm stereotypes, and although things are shifting, these are still ingrained in the workplace. Women are indoctrinated from an early age that girls are supposed to be sugar and spice and everything nice, to be pleasers, to be demure, and to mind our manners.

These gender norms are also prevalent in the workplace, where women leaders are expected to be polite, accommodating, nurturing, not to rock the boat, *and* somehow decide, direct, and execute. This tightrope of contradictions is especially tough to balance.

Women in the workplace are also saddled with—or volunteer for—non-promotable work because no one else steps up. Non-promotable work encompasses tasks that need to be done in the workplace but are not strategic or moving the organization forward. It includes things like planning the all-company party, ordering lunch, taking notes, organizing birthday recognition, keeping the supplies ordered, stocked, and organized, cleaning the break room, and tossing the food that has been in the refrigerator for weeks. It can also include projects that need to be done that may not be seen as high value.

Mary Beth Ferrante wrote about this in a *Forbes* article entitled "Do Your Feelings about Gender Roles Influence How You Manage Your Employees?" Women have a huge amount of what Ferrante calls "invisible labor." Overall, women do 2.5 times the amount of unpaid labor as men. This unpaid labor includes caregiving, chores, upkeep, and various unseen tasks, and the invisible labor doesn't just occur within the home. This invisible, unpaid labor carried out by women equals $11 trillion.[22]

Women of color face an additional burden of what is called "cultural taxation." They are expected to help more with group presentations but may not be recognized or rewarded for such activities.[23]

The question isn't who is going to let me;
it's who is going to stop me.
AYN RAND, AUTHOR (PARAPHRASE)

In her article "Organizational Wives," Diane Bergeron explains the career costs of helping: Women are expected to help, say yes, and handle a constant stream of small chores, emotional labor, and unexpected demands. Helpful women handle details, smooth over conflict, and are volunteered for task forces. They socialize new hires, advise co-workers, or show others how to use a new technology.

"As a result of giving their time, effort, and focus to organizational caregiving, women's strategic growth and progress toward their goals and high-value work may be stalled. Women often receive thank yous, and these helping behaviors do contribute to good performance reviews—but these can be faulty signals. Helping behaviors count less than core tasks regarding decisions about who gets a raise, who gets promoted, and who gets the right kinds of opportunities."[24]

When asked to do this work, negotiate for it to be a rotating job and shared or a part of the administrative responsibilities. Work on being more selective or stop volunteering when no one else is raising their hand.

You are welcome to say, "I've taken that the last three weeks; I think it's Jason's turn next," or "In order to share the responsibility of capturing takeaways from our meetings, I've pulled together a rotating schedule with a checklist." This will help distribute the load more fairly within the team.

Some key factors in finding your inner lion include using your voice to drive action, overcoming and embracing the suck of conflict and boundaries, finding ways to leverage your curiosity, and defining and setting goals with tenacity.

Amani's Inner Lion Story

Amani works in a Fortune 500 company. She initially started as a manager in the finance department. She has excellent skills and education to reach beyond her role. Plus, she has worked on a few cross-departmental projects that were instrumental in successfully implementing some fair-sized initiatives.

Amani is a heads-down, does-great-work, and doesn't-rock-the-boat kind of person. In her past organizations, she was given more responsibility (but not always more pay) because she got the work done and worked well with others. Amani will ensure her staff has the resources and covers what they need, but, at times, she hesitates to do the same for herself.

After two years in this new company, she knew she could take on more and wanted to move to the next level. She saw her peers promoted to the next level, yet she was on a different path and remained at the manager's level. Her performance appraisals were stellar, and the feedback from her leader was always appreciative and positive.

However, Amani felt stuck. Although her director supported her in the work she was performing, Amani was not sure if she supported her growth to the next level. Luckily, her leader agreed to invest in a coach (me) for Amani.

Through our work together, Amani found her voice and used it strategically. She joined the firm's employee resource group for women to get to know some other women leaders in her organization. Amani increased the breadth and depth of her network in other departments and geographic locations.

Through some of the assessments we utilized, Amani found ways to ensure her voice was heard and to focus on the key priorities of the organization, her team, and her boss, aligning her goals with each of those areas' key priorities.

Her innate curiosity served her well. She tweaked her approach to be more strategic, enhancing her communication and connection with others.

Although Amani's natural tendency is to avoid conflict like the plague, she revised the narrative in her head to view conflict as a discussion expressing different views with both parties' desire to come up with the best option for the organization. These tweaks and her curiosity helped her see things from others' viewpoints and articulate her point(s) with passion and understanding.

Amani also grew comfortable and clear about setting (and maintaining) boundaries, which led to her executing her goals.

After being promoted to director and serving just a year in that role, Amani was promoted to vice president of finance.

We Must Use Our Voice In The Workplace

Speak the truth, even if your voice shakes.
MAGGIE KUHN, ACTIVIST AND COFOUNDER OF THE GRAY PANTHERS

Find and use your voice. If not, your boss or boss's boss will most likely fail to see you in a leadership light, and you'll lack the visibility to help you move toward the next level. You have a unique perspective, and it needs to be heard.

Stop the deflection and minimization—take credit for your work. Men are generally good at this, while women leaders often have room for improvement.

You can bring light to your work without being self-serving or a blowhard. Think about why you may have difficulty sharing your success and finding ways to raise your visibility.

When you receive a compliment, don't say, "Thank you—it was really easy," or "It was nothing." Do not diminish the compliment.

I used to do this a lot—even around how I dress—and was in the habit of saying, "I got this on sale," or "I've had this for fifteen years." I didn't realize that inside and outside of the workplace, I was dismissing the compliment and not valuing the words of appreciation from someone else or what I brought to the table.

In the workplace, when someone expresses appreciation for your work, don't say, "Oh, thanks, I thought it might be helpful." Instead, be specific about recognizing its value, saying, "Thank you. I knew if we had a dashboard of key indicators on one sheet, it would drive better decision-making and execution."

When you acknowledge your value, contributions, and qualifications, leaders know you are ready for more responsibility or promotion. Focus on your overall value and articulate that value by owning it. Others want to work with those they like and trust. Claim your voice, value, and achievements—to the role, team, and organization.

Overcoming Fear And Embracing The Suck (Conflict And Boundaries)

I've been absolutely terrified every minute of my life—and I've never let it keep me from doing a single thing I wanted to do.
GEORGIA O'KEEFFE, ARTIST

We all have times when we are anxious and/or afraid. It's really about growing our courage in spite of the fear we have. Rob Gilbert talked about getting those butterflies in our stomach into formation before we move forward when it comes to fear.

Here are some key points to ponder.

Fear will always be present. It is not going to go away. That can be a good thing—we should be afraid of diving into a body of water filled with alligators or, from a work perspective, going into a meeting unprepared with a leader who is a stickler for details.

Fear lives at the edge of our comfort zone, and we must realize that we experience the most growth when we are out of our comfort zone.

Fear is afraid of action. When we move in a positive direction, even a tiny step, we shed light on that fear. Acknowledge this and move forward by taking action and exercising courage.

We can be (and often are) both fearful and courageous at the same time.

Success cannot happen without failure. Once we understand that and accept that we will step into it at some point, we will be able to overcome our fear and move forward in our careers. We learn by getting more comfortable with risk and knowing we will fail.

In his book *Practicing Greatness*, author Reggie McNeal says, "The single most important piece of information a leader possesses is self-awareness. Great leaders are self-aware."[25] Our awareness empowers us. It allows us to be intentional about how we want to show up and the decisions that can lead to the best and healthiest outcome.

Courage doesn't always roar. Sometimes, courage is the little voice at the end of the day that says I'll try again tomorrow.
MARY ANNE RADMACHER, AUTHOR

Acknowledging that fear is present can allow you to respond more effectively. Fear thrives in the darkness, and we diminish its power over us when we expose it.

We need to step back and take a healthy look at our fears. Think about how we might advise a friend to move forward in a positive direction and heed that advice ourselves. We can reduce the power that fear has over us by bringing light to it, getting curious about why we may feel that way, and then speaking the truth about it.

Women who take smart risks are more successful. Disruption is inevitable, there is uncertainty and volatility in any business today. Risk-taking is a critical skill needed to grow in your career.

We are not talking about just risk for risk's sake, but enlightened risk—do your due diligence prior to taking the leap, think about your vision of success, and take a step toward that.

According to KPMG's latest women's leadership study, women are not taking as much risk as men. Only 43 percent are willing to take the bigger risks associated with career advancement. KPMG also found that women's comfort with risk diminishes as we become more seasoned in our careers. A mere 37 percent of women with fifteen-plus years of experience were willing to take significant career-defining risks.[26]

The study by KPMG outlines that women are more likely to be less confident talking about their accomplishments, asking for a higher salary, or volunteering to do a big presentation. These are the very things that would increase their visibility and career trajectory.

Great success is achieved *with* failure. We need to see failure as a stepping stone to success. We only truly fail if we stop thinking about what we might need to tweak or change that could positively affect the outcome. We move closer to success if we welcome messing up or stepping in as a learning opportunity instead of avoiding it.

It's not that you have failed; it's that you learned something new and need to take a different approach.

Perfectionism is a myth; we will never be perfect. Providing ourselves grace when we screw up is a much healthier way to approach our lives and career. We cannot tie our self-worth to an outcome—think about what you can learn and the growth.

Speak to yourself as you would a friend. We are much harder on ourselves and speak much more harshly to ourselves than we would to a friend.

Know that each of our paths is different. What worked for others may not work for you.

Curiosity Didn't Kill The Cat—It Made Her Stronger

---

*It's daring to be curious about the unknown, to dream big dreams,
to live outside prescribed boxes, to take risks, and above all,
daring to investigate the way we live until we discover
the deepest treasured purpose of why we are here.*

LUCI SWINDOLL, AUTHOR

Coming at things from a place of curiosity can be magical. When we are genuinely curious, we become more approachable, allow folks to share their path of reasoning, vanquish defenses of ourselves and others, and help to get people on the same page. From an emotional intelligence perspective, curiosity is a valuable tool in keeping us from going down a negative path that can hinder finding out the *why*.

Some phases I invite you to try on are the following:

- Help me understand.
- Tell me more.
- I'm curious about how we got here. Can you share?

Women in the workplace are caught in between a very narrow slice of, "She's not a leader because she is too direct and alienates people" (aka a bitch) and "She is too nice, too collaborative, and won't be able to execute on the hard stuff," be it dealing with people or making tough business decisions (too soft).

When we cultivate curiosity, we diminish our defensiveness and that of others. It helps us see and understand relationships and connections among concepts and thoughts that drive ideas and creativity. This curiosity also helps our problem-solving capabilities.

Be A Goal-Digger With Tenacity

The most difficult thing is the decision to act.
The rest is merely tenacity. The fears are paper tigers.
You can do anything you decide to do.
AMELIA EARHART, AVIATION PIONEER

When you haven't set your own goals and truly, tangibly defined them, other people will do that for you based on *their* goals and desires, not *yours*. Once we have our goals defined well, we can move toward accomplishing them.

A lot of research debunks the idea of willpower to accomplish goals. Instead, grow your tenacity and put systems in place to ingrain habits. One of the ways we can grow our tenacity is to really understand and define the *why* behind the goal we set. Then, we need to get clarity around our goal.

I have a friend who each year places her goals in a small frame next to her laptop and intentionally refers to them when she starts and ends her day. It's essential to visualize your goal daily and remind yourself of why you committed to it in the first place.

It's easy for us to get off track, and it helps if we surround ourselves with people who are also goal-diggers and support us. Goal-diggers are the people who set and accomplish goals, get things done, and overcome obstacles. These are the people who are good to enlist as your accountability partner(s).

We also need to be mindful of the stories we tell ourselves and ensure that they serve us. If we continue to have negative thoughts, they become our reality. The good news is that the opposite is true.

Make sure to be clear and specific about your goals. Clarity can bring power and focus and can genuinely affect them.

We have all heard of making SMART goals: specific (clarity around what the goal actually is and what success will look like), measurable (what are the levers that will show us we have been successful?), achievable (how do we set ourselves up for success, what resources do we need?), relevant (does this goal align with the vision of my team/organization?), and time bound (what is a realistic deadline?).

It's helpful to break those goals into subgoals. Our brains are wired for progress, and when we gain momentum with the completion of the smaller tasks that help us achieve our goals, we get bursts of success, leading to overall success.

Find what motivates you and leverage that. Is it a competitor who drives you to do better or imbedding treats when you reach a milestone (like a pedicure or team lunch)? Gain inspiration from others, think about what works best for you, and leverage that.

Three Noodling Questions

1. What is one step you can take today to leverage your inner lion?

2. What do you need to do to ensure your voice is heard and that you are driven to action? What are some ways you can move toward your fear with courage?

3. How can you cultivate curiosity and be a goal digger with tenacity?

Application Box

- Use your voice: There is only one you. You have something to say, and no one in this world has the same experiences as you. Your voice is important.

- To manage fear: acknowledge, expose, and define the worst-case scenario—then determine what really is the truth. Give yourself the freedom to fail, watch the negative self-talk, and take stock of the resources you have at your disposal, the skills you bring, and the people in your corner cheering for your success.

- Leverage the power of curiosity to improve your growth and wonder. Read widely and follow what interests you.

- Ask more questions. Collect questions, not just answers.

- Stay open to new experiences. Keep a curiosity journal, travel, and try new foods that can expand your horizons.

- Set SMART goals. Surround yourself with tenacious people. Join meetups and professional groups aligned with your goals. Not only can you learn from them, but they can also provide resources and encouragement. Learn how they stay focused, what drives them, and how they get their inspiration.

7

Cultivate Influence As Your Superpower
(Secret 5)

A leader takes people where they want to go.
A great leader takes people where they
don't necessarily want to go but ought to be.
ROSALYNN CARTER, ACTIVIST AND FIRST LADY

Influence is a key tool for women to get ahead in their careers. The ability to influence is a superpower, and it can be used for good or evil.

We are focusing on the positive use of influence to grow and move your career ahead as a leader. The negative power of influence is manipulating others or utilizing power or position detrimentally.

Strong leaders understand that influence is more than power or persuasion. It is about inspiring others with a shared vision and goals and empowering others to act. Influence is using positive, productive conversations to change the way people think, feel, and act. When we enhance our capability as an influencer, we can affect the choices, opinions, outlooks, and behaviors of others.

Individuals are motivated by different things, and when we understand this, we can increase commitment and leverage performance for positive results.

We all have bosses and peers—even if we work for ourselves. The ability to influence or persuade others to support us, provide resources, or work on a project they may not be excited about will help us succeed. When we can find a way to make it a win-win and build trust, we are most effective.

We earn the right to influence; the power is not given to us. Influence doesn't necessarily equate to getting agreement; it is getting the right stakeholders to support what you are trying to achieve.

We must remember that influence requires us to become comfortable with being challenged and understand that we will not please everyone. Leadership and influence are choices. As a leader, you must make a positive impact and get results.

Julie's Influence Story

One of my past clients, Julie, works for a large hospital in Missouri and is a human resources leader. The hospital got a new CEO, Sam, and Julie's reporting relationship shifted to reporting directly to him. She also became part of the executive leadership team.

Julie already had a lot of respect from her current peers, but she needed to figure out how to improve her communication, visibility, value, and influence.

The organization was going through immense change, and not too long after her promotion, she also had to maneuver the impact of COVID-19 on all aspects of dealing with employees and the public. To my way of thinking, the top three types of workers that COVID-19 most affected were (1) healthcare workers, including mental health workers, (2) educators, and (3) human resources folks. Julie hit two out of the three.

Her influence on Sam, the CEO, was strong. She adjusted her communication style to share information in a way that was best for him to receive it: by limiting her advice to just the key facts Sam needed to know and a story of why it was necessary. She utilized a blend of thinking and emotional influence. Thus, Sam repeatedly sought Julie's advice and counsel.

Julie's advice provided the right story for Sam, enabling each issue to come to life for him. This buy-in was key since the organization faced burnout, staffing shortages, limited capacity to care for patients, and an epidemic with no real playbook to navigate the deluge of changes.

In working with the other executive leadership team members, Julie had to adjust her style to reach each of them. We worked on an influence map, whereby she focused on how each leadership team member communicated and what they needed from her. By flexing her work and communication style, she has built a strong peer rapport and gained trust with all but one peer—and he is a work in progress.

When we adjust our style, we don't want to alter who we authentically are. We don't necessarily change what we say, but the way we say it so the other person will hear us better, and we both become more successful.

Every day, we use influence, and some of us already wear capes and goggles, with persuasion as our superpower. The great thing is that influence can also be learned and grown.

So, as you think about your superhero outfit, let's get down to some concrete strategies you can add to your toolbox.

Think about a project you need to complete. One of mine is organizing four significant events/conferences for two volunteer roles in the next six months.

Think about who your stakeholders are and ask yourself the following questions:

- What is their agenda, and how can I connect it to the organization's priorities or values?
- How can I start where they are? Folks won't move far if you don't first begin where they are and help them move forward.

- What are their critical areas of concern? What are some ways I can address those concerns?
- How can I include the decision-makers as part of the process?
- Who are the people that will be on my side, and who are the ones that might be an obstacle to my success?

Once you identify your stakeholders, rank and order them. What is their level of power, and what might their needs be? Ensure you craft appropriate questions for each stakeholder group, ask questions, and then listen.

Also, consider who an ally or allies in this endeavor could be. Who may be an adjunct partner to help you be more successful? It could be a communications professional in another department or someone who can be a champion or advocate to help you leverage your influence.

An influence map is a great tool to help you be more successful. Write down the thing you want to influence in the middle of a piece of paper and circle it. Now, around the circle, write down the key stakeholder groups you must consider. Write down the key folks who need to be influenced within each stakeholder group. Think of a stoplight; have three pens ready in red, yellow, and green. If someone advocates for your project, highlight their name in green. If they are neutral, highlight yellow. If they are currently against it, highlight/underline it in red.

Next, prioritize the key stakeholders and look for those you can leverage as advocates. Who can you move from neutral to a supporter? For those who are currently green, how can you raise their support and voice for the project to help advocate for your project? For those marked in red, is there a way to mitigate their opposition or move them to neutral?

Take a look at this map and make a plan to hold conversations, prioritizing them. It's best to start with conversations that may be lower stakes and build on them. Identify why this might be important to them, utilizing the WIIFT rule to determine what's in it for them.

People do things for their own reasons, which most likely differ from those most meaningful to you. Share with your advocates how they can help you and build momentum to leverage your influence.

Once you have made your map, know it is a living document and tool that can help you navigate progress and remember whom you need to keep in contact with. Influence is not one and done; you should constantly nurture it. If you hit a roadblock, your stakeholders should know it. If there is a change, keep them in the loop. No one wants to be blindsided, and consistent feedback helps keep your stakeholders engaged. Make sure you celebrate wins, too.

Creating and utilizing influence maps can build pathways and bridges for decision-makers.

There are two key foundations of influence. The first is all about authenticity and vulnerability. There is only one *you*, and as my friend Sandra Quince says, we need to bring our *best* authentic selves to work. That means sometimes our true authentic self is not fully ready for the workplace, or we may know employees whose full authentic self does not align with the organization's core values and beliefs.

We will never have all the answers, and when we show vulnerability, we engender trust within the organization. Please note that vulnerability is not oversharing—such as recounting when our Irish wolfhound, Aberdeen, got into the Genie diaper pail advertised as "impenetrable." I won't go into details, but it involved a high-pressure hose and a vat of Dawn dishwashing liquid outside.

As a leader you don't want to overshare vulnerability with your employees, for example sharing the tape that is playing in your head, "Holy crap, I am so in over my head. What if we go off the cliff and everyone loses their jobs?"

That is oversharing and inappropriate. Get a coach if that is the case, and find a confidential outlet to help you get the resources you need to be successful or make a graceful exit.

Being vulnerable is the art of giving yourself grace and admitting you don't have all the answers. It is turning to those who know more than you do.

The second pillar of influence comes from a place of selflessness, where we focus on others' needs and balance them with our own. It's about balancing WIIFT with our needs and the organization's needs. The easiest way to find out WIIFT is to ask. If that is not an option, speak with others in their department and observe. Think through what will benefit them.

For these two pillars of influence to be successful, we need to cultivate momentum, creating a vision that paves the way for others to want to follow us. We also need to influence beliefs by painting a picture for a greater purpose, showing the *why* that inspires others. Our role as a leader is to help define the purpose and the *why*.

When you want to influence others, you must start where others are. How you show up and connect with others matters. We have all heard the golden rule: Treat others how you want to be treated. However, we are all wired differently, and if we treat folks the way we want to be treated, we will miss truly connecting with about 75 percent of people. We all have a preferred style, and instead of making that our go-to, we need to look at what is important to those we wish to influence.

I want you to toss out the golden rule and instead focus on the platinum rule: Treat others the way *they* want to be treated. If we learn to flex our style and communicate so that they can hear us better, we will all be more successful. We don't necessarily change the message, but how we say it so they can hear us better.

Once we understand the two pillars, getting into a mindset of influence is key. The mindset outline and methods below are from Andrew Neitlich, founder of the Center for Executive Coaching. He is fantastic—one of those people who is all meat and no sizzle with rich content—generous and humble. You might even think of this as a checklist with six items.

Ensure you connect authentically with the person you want to influence. Whether you need to influence a group of people or a whole organization, influence happens to one person at a time. Get advocates and champions to help you in your influence campaign.

Keep your message concise by sticking to three to five key points. Any more, and folks won't remember. Get into their shoes and think about (or ask) what's important to them or what's in it for them. People do things not because you want them to but for their own reasons. Find out what those are.

Focus on what thoughts and baggage you may bring to the discussion. Define and acknowledge any biases you need to clear beforehand, and adopt the frame of mind that would help you be most successful. As leaders, we always try to balance the triangle of relationships, results, and ego—with a preference for one or two. Be aware and intentional about the balance of these.

The last thing in cultivating this mindset is to know there is a chance/probability of failure. Have a backup plan because there are no guarantees. Do you need to take a break and come back to the conversation? There is always another way to accomplish things.

Think about your opportunity flow (influence quotient) at work. Is it a puddle in a pothole in a Walmart parking lot or a class 3 river rapid? Are you asked to be on cool projects, be your client's preferred go-to partner, or lead high-profile initiatives?

Define where you want to be and work toward growing your power base network to enhance your influence. It is crucial to balance flexibility and authenticity.

Once you know the pillars of influence, have your mindset in the right place, and your map in hand, think about which method fits the situation you need to influence.

There are some methods of influence you can utilize.[27]

Thinking

Utilize logic, facts, and three reasons for influence. We want to stick to just three reasons because most folks won't remember much more than that. The thinking brain is typically overused, but blending it with one of the other methods, especially the emotional brain, is good. An example of thinking-brain influence might be, "Our project deadline is October 31, and our vendors cannot get our supplies unless we order by the end of the day. This higher quality pipe, which is $5 more per foot, will allow us to meet our deadline and address the customer's safety concerns."

Heart

Tap into stories, imagery, and metaphors. When we use emotional influence, it can win folks over through stories that speak to the heart and through feelings and emotions. There is a lot of research about how humans believe we are using logic for decisions when our emotions actually drive the reasoning. When we paint a picture and tap into emotions, it is an intense way to wield influence. Share a story and take people on a journey using vivid images with a compelling narrative. Nonprofits utilize stories of how they've helped others to connect potential donors to their organization's mission so they can tap into a donor's time, treasure, and talents.

Firm And Flexible

What can you control, positive or negative? This is more about compliance when you want to get things done. For example, Sarah comes late to meetings. "Sarah, to get you to come on time, we will use an agenda and work to get straight to the point. I will let your supervisor know" (that can be positive or negative). This can influence Sarah to comply.

Collaboration

This method of influence uses open-ended questions but requires you to be open to what and how. Collaboration is a good way to gain commitment. It engages the heart and takes more time to invest in, showing your care by asking questions. You are flexible on how it gets achieved and in what way. An example is: "Jim, we can work together to meet this deadline. I will work on gathering the data and graphics if you build PowerPoint and logistics."

Leverage Other Influencers

Those you know and who are in your network can be leveraged through relationships and your power base. This method incorporates the influence you have established via connections and relationships you have built over time. It should be used sparingly. You make deposits into your power base by helping others, and you can later tap into this power base to request a favor (withdrawal). When using your social capital, you want to make many more deposits than withdrawals; balance doing favors with making asks when it makes sense. This leverages the relationships you have authentically built.

Big Request

This is about the *big* ask or fearless request. Who is someone amazing you would like to have in your power base? Whose work do you admire and want to connect with and build a professional friendship with? Start small and grow. This method is much easier now that we can connect with folks we admire through social media. The ability to wield influence requires big, bold ideas. Think bigger, aim higher, and own your vision.

Common Ground

Utilize the language of *we*. It taps into shared or aligned values, a common experience or belief, a similar style, etc. Another form of common ground is highlighting things we each have that make us better together. I call this the PB&J factor; we have skills that complement each other. An example might be: "I am good at the big picture, seeing a vision, and finding a common thread. Janice is great at the details of how we get there. As a team, we are well-suited for this project. We can write this book together, and it will change the world for children." Common ground is a good approach in combination with other approaches.

Think about one thing you want to influence and which of the above methods would be best. Combining some of these approaches is often best, which I call combo meal number three. When we blend thinking and heart methods, for example, we reach a larger audience, capturing both sides of the brain.

Always have a backup plan if things go south. To be most effective in influencing, utilize a combination of methods and have a plan B. We will all have face-plants and step into things. When that inevitably happens, regroup and pivot when need be.

When we stretch our influence rubber band, we go from an inner-directed to an outer-focused direction. That's how we can get traction. Find ways to practice and curate your sphere of influence.

Some additional strategies that are helpful when wanting to grow your influence include the following:

- Prepare, prepare, prepare.
- Don't strive to be interesting but to be interested in others.
- Be present.
- Ask great questions and find out what others are passionate about.
- Listen not to respond but to really understand. It shows you care and are connected, and it validates others.
- Grow your likeability—people do business with people they know, like, and trust.
- Seek to serve; do not let your own agenda get in the way of your success.
- Have a goal and be flexible with it, as well as the path you take to get there.
- Perfect your pitch short and sweet, about three minutes. First, tease out the information, then entice or please them (WIIFT), and seize (value and close with the action they take.)
- Publish your ideas; you build credibility, become known as an expert, and build your brand.
- See things from different perspectives, know there are other ways to get somewhere, keep an open mind, and get curious.

- Give people a compelling reason to do what you want them to do.
- Develop a reputation for objectivity, loyalty, and trustworthiness.
- Understand reciprocity and build credits in your power base.
- Acknowledge and validate people, respecting mutual differences.
- Cultivate your network of influential, powerful mentors and friends.
- Articulate principled arguments to those you need to influence. Keep in mind principles vary across individuals. Remember to focus on WIIFT.
- Acknowledge past leaders' success.
- Know your stuff and the pros/cons, and be seen as an expert. You also want to be generous with your expertise and become a professional resource.
- Use small wins to gain momentum.
- Connect with other people where they are. Speak their language and know what is important to them. Find a way to connect—you should know their needs and interests.

Research shows that influence is more critical for women than men in their career trajectory and leadership alignment. In a study published in *Harvard Business Review*, author Kathryn Heath found that men and women think about office power dynamics differently:

"The discrepancies help explain why women assert themselves differently.

. . .[M]en tend to talk about 'competition' when they describe office politics, using language like 'the tools people use to win at work,' whereas women are more likely to cast it as 'a natural part of influencing' and emphasize the ability to shape 'ideas and agendas.' Similarly, women and men report having differing *objectives* in the political situations they face at work. Men use words like 'achieving results,' and women talk about 'influencing others.'

In [the] study, 81% of women and 66% of men said that women are judged more harshly than men when seen as 'engaging in corporate politics.' So women don't want to be viewed as political—it undermines them. That may explain why 68% of women said they dislike office politics, even though they want to assert themselves at work—and why the majority of women in [the] interviews said they were more interested in 'influence' than in pure power."[28]

Make an impact in every single assignment that you are given.
Look at it as how can I take this to the next level.
And be confident in yourself.

MICHELE BUCK, CHAIR, PRESIDENT, AND CEO OF HERSHEY

Three Noodling Questions

1. Who did you want to be when you were younger (seventeen to twenty-three), before the world told you who you should be?

2. Who is someone you want to influence? How can you start small and grow your capabilities?

3. How can you polish yourself to be seen as an "expert"?

Application Box

- Write down the top seven to ten people who have had the greatest influence on your career thus far. Consider how they have influenced you professionally. Reach out to them to reconnect and ask what advice they may have at this point in your career.

- Determine one thing you wish to influence and create an influence map outlining key stakeholders and designating each as green, yellow, or red. Identify WIIFT as best you can. Then, choose three you can speak with to shift them to be more vigorous advocates or supporters.

- Use your power of influence for good and think about the desired outcome and where you are willing to be flexible. Also, define how you intentionally want to show up with the key stakeholders.

- Find ways to increase your expertise and be generous when sharing with others to help them grow or succeed. Become the "go-to" person for your knowledge in an area that benefits your field.

- Define your best authentic self and find opportunities to share that person in the workplace.

8

Leverage Visibility
In All Interactions
(Secret 6)

No country can ever truly flourish if it stifles the potential of its women and deprives itself of the contributions of half its citizens.

MICHELLE OBAMA, FIRST LADY AND AUTHOR

You can't get a promotion if no one knows you are there or your amazing work. Strike a balance between time at your desk working hard and collaboration with others. When opportunities arise, you must be at the forefront of the minds of the decision-makers. You need to balance nailing the core of your job while connecting and building work relationships.

When women get promoted or asked to lead significant projects, it raises our visibility.

There are clear steps you can take to raise your visibility in the workplace. You can do any one of them better to increase your growth opportunities. Visibility and ambition are not fixed assets; they can be developed over time.

Ashley's Visibility Story

One of my coaching clients, Ashley, works in a nonprofit organization. When we started our engagement, she was in mid-level leadership at a reasonably large nonprofit. She had some exposure to the organization's board of directors, but it was minimal. She desired to reach the executive director's role in her current organization or another within the same city.

I am in awe of her capabilities and accomplishments, but her title did not accurately reflect her work. Her boss leaned on her heavily, and she was doing the work of two people plus some of the CEO's responsibilities without recognition.

In our collaboration, Ashley worked on identifying key players within the organization, the board, and some of the foundations that worked with the nonprofit. She developed a plan to build relationships or further strengthen those she had. Ashley took a more active role in board meetings due to taking on a unique project on a committee with some of those key folks she had identified, and the work she did shined. Ashley started sending her boss a weekly report of projects strategically aligned with the organization's mission, showing where she could save money and serve more clients due to her team's work.

She shared her desire for growth and her ultimate goal with her boss and a board member with whom she had a good working relationship. Ashley also worked on setting boundaries and saying "no" respectfully to non-promotable or nonvalue-added work.

Within less than six months, Ashley was promoted to the second-highest level within the nonprofit and is now on track to take over the executive director's role upon her boss's retirement at year-end.

Ashley was not only nailing the core of her job, but she also identified what was needed at the next level, found ways outside her role to demonstrate her capabilities, and strengthened relationships and networks to raise her visibility. She engaged a coach on her own dime and sought additional growth opportunities to help her prepare for the next role.

I know great things are ahead for Ashley—and for you as well. To unlock and raise your visibility, choose one or two of the nine keys to enhancing visibility that follow.

Nine Keys To Enhancing Visibility

There are nine keys to unlocking the visibility of your work and of you:

Highlight The Value You Bring And Align Your Work With Your Organization's Strategic Goals

Think about how you can demonstrate value to the company. Ask your boss and your boss's boss what key things they did to grow in the firm. What classes should you take, and what professional organizations or outside activities should you connect with? Which TED Talks, recommended reading, or connecting with experts within your industry should you explore?

Find ways to think outside your job with the mindset that learning can complement your growth. Be forward-thinking; it's about your current role and how to get to the next level. Remember, sometimes we take a circuitous route that gets us exactly where we need to be.

Find Out The Key Priorities For Your Boss And Your Boss's Boss And Act On Them

Be intentional about aligning your work with their priorities where you can. If you haven't already, provide your leader with a report of the key projects in rank order and your progress. Set a regular day of the week and time to check in, review the list, and ensure you are working on your boss's, department's, and organization's priorities.

You also want to share your career goals with your boss and understand what you need to develop to reach the next level. Ask about taking on special projects that you know are aligned with the organization's strategy, goals, and values. Find ways to work collaboratively and highlight other team members.

Just like in kindergarten, we need to ensure we play well with others. You will always have people at work you do not care for. I'm not saying you must get a glass of wine or coffee with them, but you must be civil and professional.

Find ways to catch them doing something right and shine a light on it. You also want to be a promoter of others and highlight their success.

Make sure you follow through. When you commit, do everything you can to see it through to the best of your abilities. When you build a proven track record, you will be known as someone who can be counted on to bring results.

Sometimes, we will have a face-plant—or several. Take responsibility when you screw up. Remember, you have elevated visibility, which means your mistakes will, too. We all mess up and make mistakes. Learn from it, be humble, work to fix it, and engage others so you know better.

As Dr. Maya Angelou tells us, "Do the best you can until you know better. Then when you know better, you do better." When we take responsibility for our mistakes and learn from them, it demonstrates self-awareness.

Know The Numbers

How does your department make money? How does the company make money? Who are your key customers, and what are the costs and value of your products and services? Be able to speak to the value of your contribution and your worth as a leader, an employee, and a team member.

Learn what the margins are and what levers drive revenue. When you can speak to the numbers, it opens doors.

Be Intentional About How You Show Up

In board meetings, or any meetings for that matter, speak up, take risks when you see good opportunities for the organization, and step up. Schedule buffer time for meetings so you can get there five minutes early and sit in the middle of the table—not on the side, not in a corner, but where you will be seen and heard.

Watch the placement of your head. When taking notes, our heads are down, and we don't engage in the conversation. Ensure someone is designated to take notes or share the responsibility with all parties. Pay attention, even when it's not your part.

When we engage, it shows the breadth of our understanding. Speak up and ask questions. If you agree with someone else's words, say so aloud. Take small steps and grow your courage. Watch what you say and how you say it.

Remember, watch for up-speak; remove "just," "I'm sorry," etc. Also, be aware of how you physically show up. Do not shrink, and ensure you occupy an appropriate amount of space. The research Dr. Amy Cuddy did about power poses and how men take up space and women shrink is real in the workplace.[29]

In her book *Presence*, Dr. Cuddy shares how we can fake it until we become it. Learn the non-verbal expressions of power and dominance to your benefit. Our non-verbal behavior impacts both those we interact with and ourselves. Dr. Cuddy outlines a gender difference in the way women and men typically show up and participate. Women tend to make themselves smaller and take up less space; men tend to make themselves bigger and take up more space.

Be intentional about showing up and participating. Pay attention to where you sit and your posture; be more expansive and open. Make eye contact with whoever is speaking. Ask questions and make appropriate comments.

Vote For Yourself

In grade school, I ran for president of my fourth-grade class. My sister and friends helped me make signs with catchy phrases, and I picked out my favorite jeans and shirt for the big day. All my outside forces told me I would be egotistical if I voted for myself.

That morning, I shared with my mom that I was voting for Allen, my opponent. My mom got fired up: "Heidi, do you think the President of the United States votes for their opponent? Who do you think would do a better job? What is your platform, and what values do you bring to your role? Vote for yourself!"

By the way, I didn't win—but I did vote for myself and lost by just one vote.

Why would you not be in your corner? Own it, step into your power. Learn to take a compliment. Be your own cheerleader—your own biggest advocate. Know how you make a difference and how the work you do creates a positive impact and be able to speak to that value.

You are far too smart to be the only thing standing in your way.
JENNIFER FREEMAN, ACTOR

Learn And Leverage Strategic Thinking

Balance the work you do within your organization. Think about the big picture and align more with the organization's vision. Look for ways to innovate while showing appreciation for how things were done in the past. When we are solutions-focused, we communicate possibilities and potential.

Improving your communication skills is one of the best investments you can make. I want to focus on another area of communication: being thoughtful when interacting with others.

Know Your Audience And Flex Your Style To Meet Their Needs

Know in advance what you want to accomplish and prepare for what success means to you. We also know that we are all wired differently, and we need to adapt to the situation and determine the best approach. It might involve a difficult conversation with your boss, sharing disappointment with a coworker, a presentation to a group, or influencing a client.

Consider the best approach, key information to share, and the appropriate level and fit for the audience. You may want to approach your boss with curiosity, a client with WIIFT, a coworker with empathy and understanding, or another department with data. Balance confidence and humility. You also want to ensure you clearly understand their expectations of you, what you expect of them, and that you have a common understanding of what success looks like.

Build Your Relationships And Network

Your network and relationships are part of your net worth. When you spread your wings and grow your network beyond your comfort zone, you will make connections in different departments and outside the organization to those you admire in the industry. Take your connections to a different level.

One of the ways you increase your influence is through whom you are connected with. You want people to share your name to the levels above and outside your circle. The more folks know your goals, the more likely you will achieve them. Use the influence map and power-base exercise and plan who you want to connect with and bring into your circle.

Live Your Purpose And Values And Know The Purpose Of The Organization

Pay attention to your values and their connection with the organization's purpose. When you live the organization's values in your work, you act as a role model for others. Call out and recognize when others live the values within the organization. As a leader, you can encourage the team, decisions, and communication to align with organizational values.

Put yourself out there. Volunteer and show initiative for projects highlighting your strengths and capabilities that support strategic initiatives and align with your organization's purpose. Explain the value you can bring, what you can learn, and how it can benefit the company. Once you identify it, ask for it! And make sure you are successful and do a good job.

You are awesome sauce! I want you to own that. Don't follow up your accomplishments with a caveat. Share your skills and experience without saying anything negative.

Research Bears This Out

Have you told yourself or heard from others, "If I do a great job, I will get promoted, a raise, that great project, and be rewarded"? It's not enough for you to do a fantastic job. If the right people do not know about you and your capabilities, those promotions, raises, and rewards won't magically happen. In our society, women are brought up to avoid recognition and visibility—but we need to own our awesomeness.

Research by the nonprofit group Catalyst has shown that visibility in the workplace is critical for professional advancement and is the biggest differentiator between genders in the workplace when it comes to furthering their career.[30]

Research by Rob Cross, Reb Rebele, and Adam Grant, published in the *Harvard Business Review*, found that 20 to 35 percent of collaborative work is done by just 3 to 5 percent of employees (mostly women). This is the nonstrategic work that won't get you noticed.[31]

The Boston Consulting Group found that women have a disproportionate burden of housework and childcare but equally desired advancement in their careers as men. (Thank you, Captain Obvious.)[32]

Another study by New York University and Stanford scholars found that many professional women avoid taking center stage due to the barriers and biases they encounter within their organizations. In the study, women felt a pull between taking a seat at the table and being less assertive. They feared it would impair their chances of promotion if they were not cooperative, pleasant, and communal. These women adopted an "intentional invisibility" approach, a "risk-averse, conflict-avoidant" method, within their workplaces.[33]

This visibility issue is even more prevalent with the surge in remote work.

Catalyst reported increased roadblocks for women in the workplace with remote work, especially for women of color:

- One in five women reported feeling overlooked or ignored during remote meetings.
- Forty-five percent of women business leaders said it was hard for women to speak up in virtual meetings.
- One in five workers had seen discrimination in the workplace increase following the emergence of COVID-19.[34]

Find a way to highlight your accomplishments, curate advocates who speak on your behalf, and raise your visibility with those who make the decisions. When the decision-makers know your achievements due to your raised visibility, you'll have more significant opportunities for development, growth, and career advancement.

It isn't just what you know that gets you promoted; it is key that the people making promotion decisions know about your wins and accomplishments.

Three Noodling Questions

1. What can you lift up or ask others with influence to speak out about your accomplishments or wins?

2. How do you shift or amplify your brand to better align with how you want to show up in the workplace?

3. Who are some influential advocates, both within and external to your organization, who believe in you? How can you further cultivate those relationships?

Application Box ————————————————————

- Cheers to you. No one in the world has more to gain by believing in yourself and presenting your accomplishments in the workplace. Also, enlist advocates and sponsors to promote your achievements and champion your advancement.

- Focus on work aligned with the organization's mission and goals. Focus on what your boss and your boss's boss should know about the great value of your work.

- Be intentional about building your brand, voice, and how you show up in the workplace.

- Enlist advocates who will speak your name in rooms you are not in.

9

Head And Heart Are Linked To Thrive
(Secret 7)

As a leader, I am tough on myself and
I raise the standard for everybody;
however, I am very caring because I want people
to excel at what they are doing
so that they can aspire to be me in the future.
INDRA NOOYI, FORMER CHAIR AND CEO OF PEPSICO

Thriving is a state of being that we all should aspire to. Yet, everyone should clearly define what thriving means to them. However you define it, ensure it includes a blend of head and heart.

Through research and multiple interviews with women leaders across the US, I compiled a list of key skills and abilities instrumental to their career success. These skills and attributes drove their accomplishments and ability to flourish.

In order to thrive, it's essential to have clarity around your leadership style or modus operandi (MO) and define it for employees and those within the organization you work with. One way to think about it is to provide an operating manual outlining how best to work with you.

Our emotional intelligence (EI or often EQ) is the science of how we show up, connect, and communicate with others. As a leader, this is key to our success. Women typically score higher in this area than men. In our workplaces, our EQ ability empowers our capability to influence.

Cassy's Thrive Story

Over the last six years, Cassy consistently received top ratings on her performance reviews from three different leaders. She is the go-to in her department for getting things accomplished. Cassy has a gift for cutting through the noise to get to the heart of the issue and coming up with viable solutions.

Her team describes her as fair and having high expectations, and Cassy provides resources and cover for them to get projects done and be successful.

Cassy has consistently received feedback that her passion for executing the work can interfere with her relationships with colleagues in other departments. She does not suffer fools well and does not have a poker face.

This behavior was getting in the way of Cassy's moving to the next level. Cassy wanted to progress to senior director as a stepping stone to a vice president position.

After her most recent performance review, Cassy shared her frustration with Jack, one of her advocates in the organization. Jack was a straight shooter and a staunch supporter of Cassy. She had made progress for his department, which resulted in significant revenue increases.

Jack met with Cassy and suggested she work with HR to get an emotional intelligence 360-degree evaluation and a leadership coach. Jack used these tools earlier in his career and didn't want to lose Cassy to another organization. He felt this investment would help her shift perspectives and change some behaviors that were getting in her way of moving to the next level.

The HR crew knew Cassy was slotted for several succession planning roles and were eager for the organization to invest more in her development. As I was one of the coaches who regularly worked with this organization, Cassy became my client.

After we met a few times and were on our way to a trusting relationship, I brought forward the Genos 360 emotional intelligence tool. Working with HR and Cassy on which stakeholders we needed to collect feedback from, we received some tremendous actionable data to work with.

Cassy was already aware of her strengths and areas of opportunity at a high level, and when we dove into the feedback, she learned of nuances in behaviors that were blocking her next move.

Cassy dialed in on what she wanted her leadership MO to be and the key areas where she needed to shift. Once Cassy defined and wrote down an operations manual for working with her and shared it with her direct reports, she could deepen relationships, improve communications, and clarify expectations for all.

Cassy's direct reports did the same for their teams and shared the information with Cassy. It had a positive ripple effect on the other departments Cassy and her team worked with, resulting in stronger bridges among teams.

With me as her coach, she had a trusted sounding board to work through things she wanted to communicate, and she invested time in practicing pausing and gathering her thoughts before speaking.

Working through how she was perceived and how she wanted to show up allowed Cassy to be more intentional in her reactions and communication. We dove into her triggers, and Cassy put in time, focus, and work to expand her EQ capabilities.

The important thing is not to change who you authentically are as a leader but to tap into the ability to flex your style so you can meet people where they are. It's not about changing what you say but how you say it so folks can hear you better and you can all be more successful.

The comments from the 360 evaluation showed some of the skills and abilities Cassy could sharpen to enhance her leadership capabilities. With some focus and intention, Cassy could raise visibility in those areas.

Cassy was promoted to senior director in another department over a larger group within the organization. She has increased employee engagement scores and revenue by 20 percent. Cassy is currently a top candidate for two of the vice-president positions in the organization.

Define The List Of Skills And Abilities For Thriving Success

Think about your current role and the knowledge, skills, and abilities (KSAs) that have made you successful thus far. Now, think about that next level—or the role you covet in a totally different area or industry. Identify which KSAs may transfer over and what you need to leverage differently in the next role to be successful.

An example might be if you are great at sales and want to move up to director or VP of sales. The director or VP of sales skill set is a shift from your current role, and some skills and behaviors will transfer. Your ability to develop client relationships can serve you well once you lead a team of salespeople.

There are other skills you will need to acquire or leverage differently. One shift may be the focus on the team's success versus what has made you as an individual successful. It may be moving from leading others to being a leader of leaders.

What are some ways to increase your understanding of motivation, engagement, and accountability that could help the team succeed? What skills or knowledge do you need to be a leader of leaders?

Through multiple interviews of women leaders across the US, I discovered some key common skills that transcended industries, age, and title. The foundational commonality is that each of these women nailed the core of their role.

When you replace judgment with curiosity, everything changes.
ROBYN CONLEY DOWNS, AUTHOR

Successful women leaders who rise share traits and possess a combination of the following list of skills and abilities:

- Authentic and passionate about the work she does and the people she leads
- Calm under pressure
- Courageous and able to lean into discomfort, learning in the face of failure
- Has a strong sense of self, knows her own strengths and opportunities, open to feedback to improve, and knows what she brings to the table
- Has a good sense of humor and doesn't take herself too seriously
- Tenacious and makes things happen without leaving a string of casualties
- Balances compassion and accountability
- Understands relationships and how work gets executed within the organization and builds that capacity in others
- Pushes boundaries and barriers and can beat the odds
- Knows when to punt, chooses battles, and understands limited resources
- Says "yes" to the right (growth) things and no to those that don't align with goals
- Has the ability to defuse difficult situations and share tough information in a way others can hear and understand
- Does not let fear decide her fate
- Has a learner and growth mindset

- Listens well, can hear contrasting views, and is respectful, taking what works and explaining the reasoning behind decisions made to move forward
- Focuses on what is most essential
- Visionary and can see three to four steps down the road
- Communicates complex information in an easy-to-understand way
- Has high expectations and the ability to delegate
- Grows other leaders
- Rises to a challenge and can ask tough and insightful questions
- Will find the answer and not be afraid to ask for help or resources when needed
- Sees connections and can easily summarize the picture
- Takes appropriate risks and learns from mistakes
- Has worked to develop thick skin and mitigates time with naysayers
- Is transparent in communications and actions
- Provides clarity around roles and expectations
- Creates opportunities amid change and builds on success
- Can create and execute a plan during chaos
- Builds high-performing teams with a foundation of trust
- Works to get the right people and systems in place
- Makes changes as appropriate in a timely manner
- Can work with and bring together a wide variety of people, finding common ground
- Identifies talent and strengths in others and is an advocate to lift others
- Innovative and able to bring unseen options and/or solutions
- Focuses on the best and highest use of her time, delegating growth opportunities for others and providing appropriate resources for their success
- Adept at influence and negotiation to achieve end goals
- Strong understanding of key organizational stakeholders and relationships

Being self-aware is knowing who we are and how we show up . . .
It's the core of authenticity—and authenticity leads to trust.
ROBYN WARD, AUTHOR

Defining Your Leadership Modus Operandi Or MO

Typically, when the term *modus operandi* or *MO* is used, it is tied to a crime, and we automatically hear in our head the theme of our favorite detective show as we learn about the killer's MO.

In this case, think about how you want others to experience you or describe your leadership style. By defining your MO as a leader, you have clarity about your operating mode, how you work, and your method of operation and functioning. Define your leadership approach, the processes and systems you prefer, and the techniques you utilize. People desire consistency in the way they experience you as a leader.

As a leader, once your MO is defined, it helps you create an operations guide for how best to work with you and your style. You can share the operations or MO guide with those in your reporting structure, and they have a road map on how you work best.

The cool thing about this is that you help both them and you be more successful.

Once your MO is shared with your direct reports, they can create one for you and share it with the rest of the team.

Emotional Intelligence Is Your Secret Sauce

Emotions can get in the way or get you on the way.
MAVIS MAZHURA, LEADERSHIP COACH AND AUTHOR

One of the greatest investments we can make in ourselves is to work on growing our emotional intelligence as leaders. Unlike IQ, which is set, EQ can increase by up to approximately 25 percent.[35]

A favorite definition of emotional intelligence (EI) is from Dr. Ben Palmer, CEO of Genos. He shares that "EI is the science of how you show up. It is a set of skills that help us respond intelligently to emotions."[36]

Our feelings influence our thoughts, decisions, and biases in both a negative and positive aspect. Positive feelings typically broaden and build our thinking, whereas negative feelings narrow and limit our thinking.

The way we feel influences how we behave and perform. How we show up and the behavior we choose when interacting with others determines how they feel. The way they feel determines how they can engage. It affects the outcome of every relationship we have.

EI affects our thoughts, decisions, behavior, words, and tone. Our emotions are always there, and we can use them productively. Emotions are not good or bad; they just are. It is what we do with them and if we can be intentional about productively using these emotions.

EQ involves consistently responding intelligently from the heart and the head without having an immediate, nonthinking reaction. It helps us reduce the gap between how we should act and how we do. It plays out in influence, conflict management, and team effectiveness.

The brain is wired to minimize danger and maximize rewards. Our first reaction will always be an emotional one. Ninety-five percent of the time, we are unaware of our feelings.[37]

EQ is especially important when we are stressed or outside our comfort zone. Know how to manage yourself and recognize others' emotions and possible triggers so you can adjust appropriately.

As stated by Travis Bradberry and Jean Greaves, "Since our brains are wired to make us emotional creatures, your first reaction to an event is always going to be an emotional one. You have no control over this part of the process. You do control the thoughts that follow an emotion, and you have a great deal of say in how you react to an emotion—as long as you are aware of it."[38]

EQ equals decision-making, time management, change tolerance, assertiveness, empathy, stress tolerance, communication, presentation skills, anger management, trust, accountability, flexibility, social skills, and customer service.

Work on this checklist of skills and behaviors to expand your emotional intelligence capabilities:

- Practice gratitude.
- Choose curiosity over being right.
- Lead with courage and compassion.
- Watch the negative tape in your head.
- Disconnect when needed.
- Remind yourself of 7-7-7 (will this matter in seven minutes, seven days, or seven years?)
- Work on setting appropriate boundaries.
- Make sure you get enough sleep.
- Know your triggers and ask, "Who do I want to be?"
- See mistakes as learning opportunities and give yourself grace.
- Shift perspective and take a broader view.
- Center on your values and make daily choices that reflect what matters to you.

Shift Your Outlook

You can adopt some additional practices that can significantly shift your outlook, refining your approach to communication and connection with others.

Acknowledge And Let Go Of The Story In Your Head

As humans, we are hardwired for stories, and often, we fill in reasons why people do or don't do things, especially when we feel threatened. We need to let go of the judging mind. We must be willing to shift our story and open our perspective. There is a feedback loop between our thoughts and our bodies. If negative thoughts persist, so do the stressful hormones. It isn't that we're wrong, but our perceptions will be far clearer when the nervous system relaxes.

Be Here Now

Notice how and when you get triggered. It might be a change in your tone of voice, gripping sensations in your stomach, or an urge to turtle (draw into your shell). Each of us has a bodily cue and/or behavioral trigger alerting us that we feel threatened. We must decide to stay present, be curious, and explore our experiences.

Breathe

One of the best ways to stay in the present and get out of the story we are making up in our heads is to breathe. If we can pause and breathe in for four seconds and then breathe out for four seconds for three rounds, it can restore the ability to think. We are then able to respond versus react.

Acknowledge And Name Your Feelings

A useful tool Susan David, author of *Emotional Agility*, shares: When you're feeling emotional, "the attention you give your thoughts and feelings crowds your mind; there's no room to examine them." If you name your feeling, you can separate yourself from it. "Call a thought a thought and an emotion an emotion."[39]

Practice The Pause

Take time before you speak to process your emotions, which can reduce their intensity.

Track Your "Energy Log"

List what gives you energy and brings you joy. Pay attention to the things or people that drain your energy and suck away your time. Identify one change you can make right now so you're doing more of what gives you energy and less of what doesn't.

Be intentional about building through daily practices. Create stability amid times of flux and change, provide actionable feedback and seek it for yourself, and help others deal with stress by drawing on your emotional intelligence and empathy. It's really about bringing people together, leveraging their strengths, and growing their potential.

When we can come from a place of curiosity, and practice our EQ skills, we grow our strength as a leader. Defining our MO, or operational manual of how best to work with us, provides a road map for our employees to better understand our style and how best to work with us. After we take an inventory of our capabilities and review the list of skills and abilities outlined by successful women leaders, we are aware of where we want to grow and shift. Awareness empowers us.

Three Noodling Questions

1. What gives you energy, and what drains you?

2. Of the list of your KSAs (knowledge, skills, and abilities), what one(s) do you want to grow?

3. What key information do you need to provide the folks who work with/for you about your modus operandi?

Application Box

- Define what thriving in the workplace means for you.

- Review the list of skills and attributes from the data gathered from the women leaders interviewed for this book. Assess where you are now, and what key area(s) you may want to focus on.

- Develop an MO manual for working with you as a leader and share it with your team.

- Tap into an emotional intelligence 360-degree evaluation to provide clarity about how you see yourself, and how others perceive you as a leader.

- Work on a checklist and identify key areas to grow your EQ and thrive as a leader.

PART III

———

Moving Up The Ladder With Influence

10

Seek Endorsement From The Powerful

Take the tools and the skills and the resources of every kind
that you have, and go out, find something that you know
is not fair, is not just, and begin to change it.
ANITA HILL, LAWYER AND AUTHOR

There is a lot individuals can do to rise in their careers in their realm of influence. On the other hand, organizational systems and processes can also hinder growth and career development.

More women are leaving jobs to become entrepreneurs, do gig work, or even leave the workforce entirely.[40,41] This does not bode well for the growth of our workforce in companies.

There is a different approach that can be better for us all.

Workplace gender equality can be achieved when all employees enjoy equal access to compensation, benefits, rewards, resources, and opportunities.

Organizations have an incredible opportunity to engage and develop their women leaders. We cannot change the systems as individuals, but a focus within the organization can.

Review pay and compensation to make strides and progress toward gender equity in pay and opportunities. Research shows that approximately 42 percent of women have not asked for a raise. Of those in the US who have asked for a raise, 79 percent have received some form of increased compensation.[42]

Workplaces must provide equal pay for work of equal or comparable value, removing obstacles and barriers that keep women from equal and full participation in the workforce.

There are three key ways to work toward equitable compensation. First, conduct a thorough pay audit. Some great consulting firms in the US specialize in pay equity. Second, embrace transparency of compensation throughout the organization. Third, women should be empowered through recognition programs. Be intentional about high-profile projects, ensuring a mix of genders.

According to research, three in ten women believe there is a significant gender gap in compensation.[43] Part of that impact is due to childcare challenges and a more significant expectation on women to care for kids and the elderly.[44]

In the United States, women represent only 48% of employees entering the corporate workforce. When the time for first promotions to manager comes around, only eighty-one women are promoted for every 100 men.[45] This is often referred to as the broken rung of the career ladder.

Women feel men have an easier time with career progression. Approximately 49 percent of women have experienced either direct or indirect sexism and or unconscious bias in their organizations.[46]

For recognition and support, organizations can provide formal and informal mentorship and network opportunities. Cultivate a strong group of advocates in the senior leadership ranks to be proponents for women leaders. Have the role of advocate be part of senior leadership woven into performance expectations.

Provide development for all people managers, including unconscious bias training and how to offer and receive specific, actionable, and fair feedback to both genders.

Build performance reviews and feedback around objectively measurable criteria. This especially helps employees who work remotely or on hybrid schedules.

Instill a culture of inclusion, well-being, and belonging. Work-life balance is really an outdated term. Now, it is more about work-life integration. Organizations will benefit from results-based work productivity versus using measures such as butts in seats or hours seen in the office.

Women desire flexibility in the workplace. According to the McKinsey 2023 study, 80 percent of women are looking for jobs and organizations that provide flexibility to have work-life integration.[47] More than three-quarters of women in the workplace would like to work remotely in some capacity.[48]

Women are 24 percent less likely to be offered advice from a senior leader than men. This lack of support contributes to their being held back from advancement.[49]

Organizations can focus on three key things to increase well-being and a sense of belonging within the workplace. First, provide flexibility in as many positions as possible. Second, ensure that leadership models and is accountable for living the culture and supporting the growth of women in leadership. Third, the initiatives within the organization must be instilled and measured.

As of this book's publishing, most Fortune 500 companies offer inclusive benefits that include their LGBTQIA+ employees. Ninety-one percent have nondiscrimination policies that include sexual orientation and gender identity. Seventy-seven percent of the Fortune 500 companies provide transgender-inclusive benefits.[50]

Organizations can provide informal and formal mentorship programs. They can also offer a strong sponsorship focus and build a culture of advocacy. Sponsors utilize their positions of influence to advocate for the advancement of female leaders.

Developing support and expectations for male leaders to become allies, advocates, and sponsors of women leaders is vital in building the organization's bench of women leaders.

Providing resources and budgetary support for women in the organization to join female-led professional organizations allows women to strengthen their leadership capabilities and network and receive support from others to take on more significant leadership roles.

Organizations must provide professional development funds to partner with a leadership coach.

Women tend to get asked to deliver rather than develop a vision. To shift to broader leadership roles, encourage female leaders to focus strategically on organizational operations.

There are questions you can ask women to help nurture and cultivate a strategic vision. Examples include: What is your vision for the organization, and how does it fit into the bigger picture? Who are the stakeholders to include in developing this vision? What are some tactical and operational aspects of the organization you need to have a firmer grasp of? What areas of expertise do you need to grow?

Ideas for male leaders in your organization or senior female leaders to support emerging female leaders include the following:

- Ensure all leaders have equal access to all crucial information.
- Be equitable with all employees in assessing both current capabilities and potential capabilities.
- In meetings, call on a woman first. Ensure equal airtime between male and female voices in conversations.
- When a man interrupts a woman, respectfully call it out.
- When a man takes credit for something a woman did or repeats a good idea recently shared by a woman, acknowledge it.

- When "nonpromotable" tasks must be accomplished, ensure both genders are volunteering/"voluntold" to complete the work through equal rotation. Nonpromotable tasks might include organizing parties, serving on lower-ranking committees, or running errands.
- Utilize the "flip it to test it mentality" to reduce bias criticism. When someone makes a comment or statement believed to be gender biased, reverse the gender. "He will not return to work after having this child." "He should smile more." "Kyle has prostate cancer and cannot fulfill his job duties."

Focusing on equity and transparency and committing resources for development will go a long way in increasing the number of leadership opportunities for women.

Three Noodling Questions

1. What does your organization currently do to support women leaders? How can it be expanded?

2. How do you influence increased pay transparency in your organization? Can you share other companies' best practices?

3. How can you help your leader provide more specific actionable feedback for your growth?

Application Box

- Invest in and support a women's employee resource group (ERG).

- Do a pay audit and be transparent about pay.

- Make taking smart risks safe for both genders.

- Ensure your organization provides fair, specific, actionable feedback to all employees.

- Offer paid parental leave to all parents.

- Acknowledge that men and women have different workplace experiences.

11

Eat The Elephant
One Bite At A Time

I am not afraid. I was born to do this.
ATTRIBUTED TO JOAN OF ARC, MILITARY LEADER

The best part about your story is that the next page is blank, and you get to write it. You are the architect of your career.

When you determine your true values, you help define what success looks like for you. Defining each area of your life of wealth goals is key. What is important for your financial wealth, your social or status wealth, your freedom or time wealth, and your physical health wealth?

Where are you now, and where do you want to be? Yes, we must nail the core of our current position and focus on what's next.

Now comes the work of becoming crystal clear about your priorities. The hard part is that it can limit options, and the wonderful part is that you can laser-focus on reducing your what-ifs to *what's possible*. Commit to what is essential to you.

As children, we hear the word *no* about four hundred times per day. As adults, we tend to avoid asking if there is a chance the answer is no.

We may not initially reach the goal we want, but most certainly will not if we don't ask.

What are you holding back? Where can you raise your voice and start speaking up? Ask for a raise, go after a stretch position, go back to school, speak up in a meeting where you have typically been quiet, and ask advice from someone you admire.

Remember, there's a special place in hell for those women who don't help other women. Lift others as you grow in your career. Be the spark that ignites a flame in the lives of others.

The success of every woman should be the inspiration to another. We should raise each other up.

SERENA WILLIAMS, ATHLETE AND ENTREPRENEUR

Tap into resources that can aid your journey. There are so many; the following are a few:

- Join professional organizations and work toward a leadership role. The networking opportunities are boundless.
- Connect with female leaders you admire and learn about their journeys. Share your goals. Ask how you can help them.
- Build a strong heart hive that is a sounding board for you. Help each other grow and develop in your careers.
- Tap into development offered and paid for by your organization. Upon completion, teach the material back to your team.
- Engage a coach who works with female leaders.
- Do a deep dive into one of the seven secrets to grow your capabilities.
- Attend and join conferences that are targeted to growing women in leadership.
- Be intentional about your visibility at work. Use your voice.

For several years, I've spoken at state and regional conferences about being the chief executive officer of your career. Others will design your desired career for you if you do not design your desired career. It is up to you to take charge.

The wonderful thing about being CEO of your own career is that you are in charge. That also can be pretty scary. Think back to your first job. What strengths did you show early on that you still use today?

Your energy introduces you before you even speak. Be your authentic self. Step up and know you can do amazing things.

How do you define credibility? Assess where you are now and specify where you would like to be. Ask people you respect how they would describe you and your strengths in the workplace. We judge ourselves by our intent and lens; knowing how others see us is essential. We can become aware of our strengths and potential gap(s).

Credibility typically assesses if someone is/has:

- Trustworthiness
- Competence
- Consistency
- Authenticity
- Respectfulness
- Accountability
- Loyalty
- Honesty and integrity

What are one or two things you can do that will enhance your credibility at work?

Know your strengths, when you might be prone to overuse those strengths, and how to bring folks onto your team who complement where you could be stronger. Remember, our strengths can serve us as well as get in our way.

Shift your mindset to see feedback as a gift. We cannot grow if we are not aware of how we can improve. Every individual has weaknesses that can impede success. Once aware, we can mitigate and overcome those barriers.

Work and life are all about relationships. By growing our emotional intelligence and understanding our triggers, we can be more intentional about how we want to engage and show up.

Keep well-rounded relationships in the workplace. Think of a big X on the left tip as the relationship with your boss, the bottom right as the employees you manage (or others for whom you direct the work), the top right tip as the working relationship with peers, and the bottom left as clients or customers, both internal and external. It is imperative to manage relationships in those key stakeholder groups.

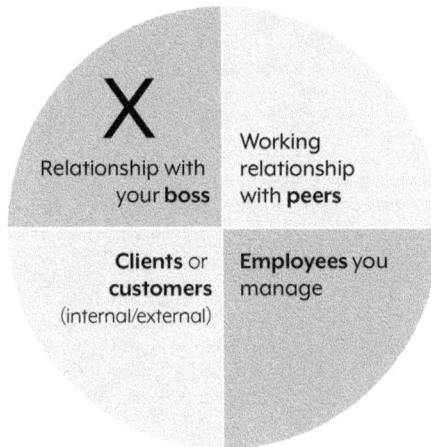

Details matter, and focus on the 80/20 rule (unless you are in finance). The 80/20 rule, also known as the Pareto Principle, used mostly in business and economics, states that 80% of outcomes result from 20% of causes.

Be strategic and understand the key goals and levers that drive your firm and industry. Get outside of your area of work and learn about other areas of the organization.

Tap into those who can help you grow. Who are your mentors, and is there an area that is missing? Do you have advocates and champions who say your name in rooms you are not in? Do you need to enlist a coach to grow your career?

Make sure you take care of yourself. You cannot pour from an empty vessel and care for others if you do not meet your needs.

Three Noodling Questions

1. Who is someone you can connect with or reach out to who can help you grow in your career?

2. What do you need to let go of so you can focus on the priorities you have defined?

3. Where is the best place to start from where you are now? How can you take one step this week?

Application Box ———————————————————

- Define the stakeholders you must manage (boss, peers, employees, clients, or customers).

- Tap into resources that work for you. Remember to stretch your rubber band. We grow most when we are in a place of discomfort.

- Take action to outline your key priorities and what's next for you. If you don't, others will define that for you.

12

Into The Leadership Future

*I don't want to get to the end of my life
and find that I just lived the length of it.
I want to live the width of it as well.*

DIANE ACKERMAN, POET

Think about the bench test—sitting on a bench, reflecting on the entirety of your life.

At the end of your life, what has really been important?

What are your most proud moments and accomplishments? How would others describe your impact and influence during your time on earth? Does it align with your values and goals?

Clarity, direction, intentionality, and tenacity will get you there.

In *Alice's Adventures in Wonderland*, Lewis Carrol has a great exchange between Alice and the Cheshire Cat.

"Would you tell me, please, which way I ought to go from here?" asks Alice.

"That depends a good deal on where you want to get to," said the Cat.

"I don't much care where—" said Alice.

"Then it doesn't matter which way you go," said the Cat.

"—so long as I get somewhere," Alice added as an explanation.

"Oh, you're sure to do that," said the Cat, "if you only walk long enough."[51]

We all have a limited amount of energy and focus, and there are 187 things trying to capture our attention at any single moment in our lives.

From a career perspective, what do you want to accomplish? Which of the seven secrets will benefit you the most? Is it the one-two punch or combo meal number three? Where should you concentrate your focus and energy to be most beneficial?

Secret 1: The *Real* You—The State Of Becoming

What is your why or your purpose? Get down to the core of what is important to you. By defining the core values that drive you (no more than seven), you can show up and lead in a way that aligns with your values and purpose. This is your true north.

If we do not define who we are, what we stand for, and what we want, others will define those things for us. Society has painted a picture of success: a fancy car, certain clothes, hair, weight, look, status, etc. What is *your* definition of success? Be specific, concrete, and true to what is important to you.

Once that is defined, we can design our careers to mirror it. Who do you want to become? What are your core values and true north?

We all have areas where we are strong and areas where we are not gifted. It isn't about having it all. Success in the workplace is playing to your strengths, shoring up your weaknesses so they do not derail you, and building a team that can cover the capabilities you need to succeed.

Understanding your workplace leadership style is essential. When we understand what drives us, we know what we need to be successful. As a leader, it is imperative to understand the drives and needs of others as well. We all can be more successful when we tap into the platinum rule of treating others how they prefer to be treated.

Learn the work style and communication preferences of those above you. Not only your boss but the level above your boss. How do they answer questions, keep folks on an even keel, react when things are not going well, and share stories to get their point across? Then, think about the parts you may want to adopt. Keep notes about not only those you admire but also behaviors or styles that you know are not a fit for what you want as your leadership MO.

How do you flex your communication style to leverage the strengths of your employees, peers, and leaders?

Secret 2: Curate Your Heart Hive To Align With Your Vibe

What is your leadership brand? Are you living it, and would your team and other stakeholders define it in the same way?

Smart networking connects you to incredible opportunities. Planting seeds and helping others get what they need boomerangs back to you. Ensure you continue cultivating your network's curation and growth; it is essential to your success.

Who are your team of mentors, and do they serve different parts of your career growth that truly benefit you? Do they include those who challenge you and stretch your capabilities?

Who are the advocates in your corner who provide the support you need? Most importantly, who is your champion who will speak your name in rooms you are not in that will set you up for opportunities and growth?

The five people you spend most of your time with greatly influence your growth. Are your five serving you? Remember, if you are the smartest person in the room, you're in the wrong room.

Secret 3: Fail Your Way To Success

The only true way you fail is to stop trying. How can you embrace mistakes as learning opportunities? Instead of beating yourself up when you screw up, say to yourself, "Well, that didn't go as planned." Then ask, "What do I need to learn from this?"

When we shift from a fixed mindset to a growth mindset, many more options are open and available. The intentionality of changing to what is possible will serve our career aspirations and our lives outside of work as well.

Expand your horizons. Where can you be bolder and play bigger? You have amazing ideas that need to be shared and explored so that your organization can benefit from them. Don't wait until they are fully baked; share them and let others help you flush them out.

Part of being bolder is getting more comfortable with risk. It's about being OK with being uncomfortable and moving forward. What is something that is holding you back, and how can you move forward? Who can you get in your corner to help you?

The other *f* word is *feedback* (positive or negative). What if you shifted your idea of feedback to being a gift? Many of us see it as criticism. It really is just the opinions of others regarding something we have shared. Just like a gift, we can either receive it and thank whoever shares it or not incorporate it. You decide if it will improve your idea or you in some way or not. Take what you need and leave the rest.

Secret 4: Find Your Inner Lion

Use your voice. There is only one you, with your knowledge, skills, abilities, and outlook. Your voice is crucial and needs to be heard. No other human has the same lens and experience as you.

It can be scary to put yourself out there, and you cannot be authentic unless you do. Taking action can reduce our fear. Using our voice despite fear is courage. Who can support you through this? Who can chime in and amplify your voice and ideas in meetings?

Curiosity didn't kill the cat; it made her stronger. One of my four core values is curiosity. It serves as a positive driver in almost every area of life. Being more curious can improve your influence capabilities and relationships. Where can you bring genuine curiosity to serve you better? How can you enhance your open-ended questions and really listen?

We have to learn to embrace the suck and get more comfortable with conflict. Conflict is not a dirty word; it is prevalent in every organization. This isn't the same as anger or being threatened—it is about respectful disagreement.

When you experience conflict at work, how can you stay in discomfort and use your voice and influence to express your ideas?

Be a goal-digger. Set goals for yourself and execute them. Break them into milestones, find support, and farm out the parts you are not good at (or don't have time for). We have one life on this earth. You have already outlined what success looks like, and setting and executing goals is how you get there.

What support do you need to achieve your goals? Who can you enlist to help you get there? What resources do you need? What is one step you can take today to move forward? Use your voice and ask for help.

Secret 5: Cultivate Influence As Your Superpower

Influence is how work gets done within organizations. First, no matter who you influence, you must start where they are. People move or act based on what is important to them. Understanding their communication style and how to flex yours to communicate what's in it for them leverages your success.

Humans are wired for stories. Our success rises when we share a compelling story that aligns with what we are trying to influence.

How can you enhance your influence capabilities? Coming from a place of curiosity can help ascertain where people are so you have a starting place. What is one step you can take to improve your ability to tell engaging stories? Can you create a "bank" of stories to pull from when needed?

Secret 6: Leverage Visibility In All Interactions

As reported by Catalyst, visibility is the number one differentiator for gender career progression in the workplace. It is imperative to leverage your visibility to rise in your career trajectory.[52]

Your energy shows up before you speak. Think about yourself as a brand. How do you want others to experience you at work? What is important to you? Does it embody your core values and your goals? Is it authentic?

How can you enlist advocates to enhance your visibility? Who says your name in the rooms you're not in? Do they wield influence?

Get noticed by the boss and above. How can you be more intentional about having strategic conversations with higher-level leadership that align with the organization's vision and key goals?

Sit in the front row, ask questions, and be strategic where you sit in meetings. Use your voice and support other women when they speak up.

Secret 7: Head And Heart Are Linked To Thrive

What are the skills or abilities where you shine? Are you aware of areas that are opportunities for you? How can you shore those up? Do you understand the impact of your leadership style (leadership MO)? What might become commitments to growing and honing your emotional intelligence capabilities?

Bonus question: What can you leverage to influence your organization's systems to be more inclusive and equitable?

What rules work or do not work for you within the organization?

The worst advice I ever received was to follow the rules.
The truth is when you follow the rules, you're perpetuating the
status quo. It propelled me to create a career that has been all
about breaking the rules that don't make sense.
SHELLEY ZALIS, CEO, THE FEMALE QUOTIENT

Her Rise Her Rules includes several stories from amazing women leaders whom I've interviewed and coached over the years. You may be in a different season of life or a different place.

You will face obstacles and challenges. Not everyone will like you—you won't be their cup of tea or shot of whiskey, and that is okay. You don't even like everybody.

What rules will help you rise in your career? What outlook will serve you best?

I promised myself this book would be in your hands by the end of 2024, come hell or high water.

In July 2024, during my annual mammogram checkup, the technician and doctor found something concerning. It ended up being cancer.

After I got the news and shared it with Chris, my spouse, I had two-plus Moscow mules and floated in the pool instead of eating dinner. Then, I shared the news with our two daughters.

I opted for a more aggressive approach to reduce the chances of the cancer's recurrence. In September 2024, I had a double mastectomy, and they ended up finding cancer in the second breast.

The great news is that the doctors believe they got all the cancer, and I'm healing well.

Life does not always go as we plan. I like to jump up after a knockdown, say, "Plot twist!" and then decide how best to move forward. We are in charge of our outlook.

You have your own story and get to write it in a way that is best for you. I hope you take what works for you to help you rise . . . and leave the rest.

Please know I am in your corner, cheering you on!

Just like moons and suns.
With the certainty of tides.
Just like hope springing high.
Still I'll rise.

MAYA ANGELOU, POET

Three Noodling Questions

1. Where do you go from here? What is one step you can take toward that goal?

2. Who can you enlist to help you share this journey?

3. What resources can you tap into to move yourself forward?

Application For You ─────────────────────

- What would you do if you knew you had less time—a decade or just a few years to live your life? You may have less time than you think. Are you ready to learn the truth about yourself? What truths are you holding inside? What would you say about your life at the end of your life?

- We can give ourselves and others grace while also holding ourselves accountable.

- When you cultivate your dreams, they become decisions. Be mindful of whom you spend time with. Iron sharpens iron. You get to define your Heart Hive.

- It is not selfish to do what is best for you.

- The same boiling water that softens the potato hardens the egg. It's about what you're made of, not circumstances.

- The world needs who you were made to be. Listen to your inner mentor (rather than your inner critic) about who you truly are.

You are *AWESOMESAUCE* and in a state of becoming.

You are the architect of your career. Who do you want to be as a leader?

Go be it!

Acknowledgments

My heart is filled with gratitude for all the help and voices that supported me and allowed this book to be.

Firstly, to the one hundred plus women I've interviewed and coached who brought their voices and shared their time and stories with me: I am forever grateful for your generosity.

A huge thank you to Mark LeBlanc, my business coach; Henry DeVries, CEO of Indie Books International; and the amazing Indie Books International team, whose encouragement, prodding, and keen eye kept me moving forward (albeit more slowly than I planned!).

To Kelly Bonnallie, the marketing maven full of wonderful ideas, and Jessica TeRuki, a photographer and artist extraordinaire: thank you both!

I appreciate the support of my two best friends—Alison Anthony (who is also a gifted editor!) and Maureen TeRuki—throughout this labor of love and bane of my existence—researching and writing over five years.

I am so grateful to my parents, Tex and Ellen Hartman, for their love and for instilling kindness and social justice's importance in their four kids. The world is better for your being in it.

Last, and most importantly, love and thank you to Chris, who keeps me centered and laughing, and our two amazing, clever, beautiful, and funny daughters, Katie and Meg.

About The Author

People who know Heidi Hartman will first tell you that she gives the best hugs in the world. They will also likely share that she is a unique combination of fierce loyalty, a great sense of humor, and tenacity. They also know that with more than two decades of experience in corporate leadership development and human resources, Heidi champions women leaders.

Heidi is dedicated to transforming "what ifs" into what's possible with tangible successes through strategic adaptability, emotional intelligence, and an engaging approach. As the head of the Heidi Hartman Consulting firm, she gets results for her clients with personalized coaching and insightful consulting to help women overcome barriers and achieve their professional and personal goals. Heidi's expertise lies in leadership coaching and building high-performance teams and organizations, but her superpower is really seeing each individual and helping identify a pathway for authentic leadership success. Heidi's mission is to empower women to achieve unprecedented career growth, team success, and a vibrant workplace culture.

As a speaker, Heidi presents to women in leadership nationwide, leaving them laughing and armed with hope and pragmatic tools to achieve their dreams. Several nonprofit boards are proud to have (or had) Heidi as a board member, including United Way (chairing Women United), International Coaching Federation, YWCA, whose mission is to Eliminate Racism and Empower Women, and Society for Human Resource Management Oklahoma—as State Director.

Heidi is a constant learner. She has a master's in human relations with a focus in organizational dynamics from the University of Oklahoma and has studied at Oxford. She has an alphabet soup of certifications: SHRM-SCP, SPHR, Certified Executive Coach, Certified Emotional Intelligence Practitioner, Insights Discovery LP, and a yellow belt in Lean Six Sigma.

Heidi laughs easily and often, never taking herself too seriously, but she gives her work and family her full devotion. She grew up in the Midwest, married her best friend Chris, and raised two smart and funny daughters, Katelyn and Megan. They live with cats Buckminster Fuller and Korn, who are shepherded by Mowgli, the Aussie dog.

Works Cited And Author's Notes

1   McKinsey & Company, "Women in the Workplace 2024," p. 11, accessed February 6, 2025, https://www.mckinsey.com/featured-insights/diversity-and-inclusion/women-in-the-workplace.

2   McKinsey & Company, "Women in the Workplace 2024," p. 37.

3   Tim Hellwig, "The diversity of the top 50 Fortune 500 CEOs over time," *Medium*, August 21, 2023, https://medium.com/@timhellwiguw/the-diversity-of-the-top-50-fortune-500-ceos-over-time-88c29f796cc8.

4   Jim Sliwa, "Women Now Seen As Equally As Or More Competent Than Men," *American Psychological Association*, July 18, 2019, https://www.apa.org/news/press/releases/2019/07/women-equally-more-competent.

5   Juliana Menasce Horowitz, Ruth Igielnik, and Kim Parker, "Women and Leadership 2018," Pew Research Center, September 2018, www.pewresearch.org/social-trends/2018/09/20/women-and-leadership-2018/.

6   "Survey Shows Changing Attitudes about Women's Intelligence," *Harvard Health Publishing*, November 1, 2019, https://www.health.harvard.edu/mind-and-mood/survey-shows-changing-attitudes-about-womens-intelligence.

7   Sharon R. Cohany and Emy Sok, "Trends in Labor Force Participation of Married Mothers of Infants." Monthly Labor Review, February 2007, https://www.bls.gov/opub/mlr/2007/02/art2full.pdf.

8   Mary Whitfill Roeloffs, " How Valuable are Stay-at-Home Parents? They Do About $4,500 of Unpaid Labor Per Month, New Study Says," *Forbes*, April 19, 2024, https://www.forbes.com/sites/maryroeloffs/2024/04/19/how-valuable-are-stay-at-home-parents-they-do-about-4500-of-unpaid-labor-per-month-new-study-says/.

9   Kathy Gurciek, "Flexible Work Options, Career Development Can Keep Women In the Workplace," *SHRM*, March 8, 2021, https://www.shrm.org/topics-tools/news/inclusion-diversity/flexible-work-options-career-development-can-keep-women-workplace.

10   Ana Júlia Calegari Torres, et al., "The Impact of Motherhood on Women's Career Progression: A Scoping Review of Evidence-Based Interventions," *Behavioral Sciences (Basel, Switzerland)* 14, no. 4 275. 26 Mar. 2024, doi:10.3390/bs14040275.

11   Emma Hinchliffe, "The Share of Fortune 500 Companies Run by Women CEOs Stays Flat at 10.4% as Pace of Change Stalls," *Fortune*, June 4, 2024, https://fortune.com/2024/06/04/fortune-500-companies-women-ceos-2024/.

12   Julie Coffman, Andrea D'Arcy, Erin Grace, and Krystie Jiang, "Beyond Leadership Behaviors that Propel Women to the Top," Bain and Company, accessed March 5, 2025, https://www.bain.com/insights/beyond-policies-leadership-behaviors-that-propel-women-to-the-top/.

13   Insights Discovery, accessed March 5, 2025, https://www.insights.com/us/.

14   Adam Grant, *Give and Take: Why Helping Others Drives Our Success* (Penguin Books, 2014).

15   Carol S. Dweck, *Mindset: The New Psychology of Success* (Ballantine Books, 2007).

16   David S. Yeager, and Carol S. Dweck, What Can Be Learned from Growth Mindset Controversies? *American Psychologist* 75, no. 9 (2020), 1269–1284, https://doi.org/10.1037/amp0000794.

17   Elena Doldor, Madeleine Wyatt and Jo Silvester, "Research: Men Get More Actionable Feedback Than Women," *Harvard Business Review*, February 10, 2021, https://hbr.org/2021/02/research-men-get-more-actionable-feedback-than-women.

18   Paola Cecchi-Dimeglio, "How Gender Bias Corrupts Performance Reviews, and What To Do About It," *Harvard Business Review*, April 12, 2017, https://hbr.org/2017/04/how-gender-bias-corrupts-performance-reviews-and-what-to-do-about-it.

19   Elena Doldor, et al., "Research: Men Get More Actionable Feedback than Women."

20   Emily Crockett, "The Amazing Tool that Women in the White House Used to Fight Gender Bias," Vox, Sep 14, 2016, https://www.vox.

com/2016/9/14/12914370/white-house-obama-women-gender-bias-
amplification.

21 Therese Huston, *How Women Decide: Everyone's Watching You Call the
    Shots. Here's How to Make the Best Choices* (HarperOne, 2017).

22 Mary Beth Ferrante, "Do Your Feelings about Gender Roles Influence How
    You Manage Your Employees?" *Forbes*, August 30, 2022, https://forbes.
    com/sites/marybethferrante/2022/08/30/do-your-feelings-about-gender-
    roles-influence-how-you-manage-your-employees/.

23 "Cultural Taxation: This Hidden Burden is Holding Back Black Female
    Leaders," Thewesuite.com, February 5, 2025, https://www.thewiesuite.
    com/post/cultural-taxation-the-hidden-burden-holding-back-black-
    female-leaders.

24 Diane Bergeron, "Organizational Wives: The Career Costs of Helping Out,"
    Chief Talent Officer, May 17, 2023, https://chieftalentofficer.co/2023/05/17/
    organizational-wives-the-career-costs-of-helping-out/.

25 Reggie McNeal, *Practicing Greatness: 7 Disciplines of Extraordinary Spiritual
    Leaders* (Jossey-Bass, 2006).

26 2019 KPMG Women's Leadership Study, "Risk, Resilience, Reward," *KPMG*,
    2019, https://assets.kpmg.com/content/dam/kpmg/lv/pdf/2019/03/KPMG_
    Womens_Leadership_Study.pdf

27 Andrew Neitlich, "Certified Powerbase and Influence Coach,"
    (certification course) Center for Executive Coaching, 2018, https://
    centerforexecutivecoaching.com/about/

28 Kathryn Heath, "3 Simple Ways for Women to Rethink Office Politics and
    Wield More Influence at Work," *Harvard Business Review*, December 18, 2017,
    https://hbr.org/2017/12/3-simple-ways-for-women-to-rethink-office-politics-
    and-wield-more-influence-at-work.

29 Amy Cuddy, "Your body language may shape who you are," TEDGlobal,
    June 2012, https://ted.com/talks/amy_cuddy_your_body_language_may_
    shape_who_you_are.

30 Heather Foust-Cummings, Sarah Dinolfo, and Jennifer Kohler, "Sponsoring
    Women to Success," Catalyst, 2011, assets.catalyst.org/7a7504c2-3ea0-
    47a5-9f92-b25401415091/catalyst-web-document-report-sponsoring-
    women-to-success_Original%20file.pdf.

31 Rob Cross, Reb Rebele, and Adam Grant, "Collaborative Overload,"
    Harvard Business Review, January–February 2016, https://hbr.org/2016/01/
    collaborative-overload.

32 Jennifer Garcia-Alonso, Matt Krentz, Deborah Lovich, and Stuart
    Quickenden, "Lightening the Mental Load that Holds Women Back,"
    BCG Global, April 10, 2019, https://bcg.com/publications/2019/lightening-
    mental-load-holds-women-back.

33 Swethaa Ballakrishnen, Priya Fielding-Singh, and Devon Magliozzi,
    "Intentional Invisibility: Professional Women and the Navigation of
    Workplace Constraints," *Sociological Perspectives* 62, no. 1, June 25, 2018,
    https://doi.org/10.1177/0731121418782185.

34 Catalyst, "Make the Invisible Visible: Catalyst #BiasCorrect for International
    Women's Day 2021 Campaign Asks Challenging Questions," news release,
    accessed February 13, 2025, https://catalyst.org/fr/about/newsroom/2021/
    bias-correct-iwd.

35 Paula Thompson, "EQ vs IQ: The Unexpected Edge That Changes
    Everything," ENotAlone.com, January 22, 2025, https://www.enotalone.
    com/article/personal-growth/eq-vs-iq-the-unexpected-edge-that-
    changes-everything-r21832/.

36 Marie El Daghl, host, *Emotional Intelligence at Work*, podcast, season
    1, episode 0, "What Is Emotional Intelligence? Dr Ben Palmer Breaks It
    Down to Marie El Daghl," Genos International, March 30, 2021, https://
    genosinternational.com/emotional-intelligence-at-work-podcast/what-is-
    emotional-intelligence-dr-ben-palmer-breaks-it-down-to-marie-el-daghl/
    transcript-season-1-episode-0/.

37 Tasha Eurich, *Insight, The Surprising Truth About How Others See Us, How
    We See Ourselves, and Why The Answers Matter More Than We Think*, (Crown
    Currency, 2018).

38 Travis Bradberry and Jean Greaves, *Emotional Intelligence 2.0* (TalentSmart,
    2009), pp. 16–17, as quoted in Dariusz Łukasik, "Emotions and Their
    Impacts on Our Lives," Dare to Live (blog), September 1, 2023, https://
    daretolive.blog/2023/01/09/emotions-and-their-impact-on-our-lives/.

39 Amy Gallo, "How to Control Your Emotions During a Difficult
    Conversation," *Harvard Business Review,* December 1, 2017, https://hbr.
    org/2017/12/how-to-control-your-emotions-during-a-difficult-conversation.

40 Soutik Biswas, "Why female entrepreneurs are key to getting more women
    to work," *BBC*, October 28, 2024, https://www.bbc.com/news/articles/
    c4g0g5005ggo.

41 John Dujay, "Why are more women leaving their jobs than men?"
    Insurance Business, October 24, 2022, https://www.insurancebusinessmag.

com/us/business-strategy/why-are-more-women-leaving-their-jobs-than-men-424968.aspx.

42 Emma Burleigh, "Some women don't ask for pay raises because they are afraid of the consequences," *Fortune*, March 8, 2024, https://fortune.com/2024/03/08/why-women-dont-ask-for-pay-raises/?taid=65eb8cc2bf5ae10001702fb8.

43 Patricia Mendoza, "Is the gender pay gap real? Survey shows divide among Americans," App.com, March 9, 2025, https://www.app.com/story/news/2025/03/09/gender-pay-gap-study-talkerresearch-2025/81761945007/.

44 Ashleigh Popera, "The Gender Pay Gap: Addressing Systemic and Modern Challenges," *Enterprise Solutions*, March 6, 2025, https://www.shrm.org/enterprise-solutions/insights/gender-pay-gap-addressing-systemic-modern-challenges.

45 Kweilin Ellingrud, Lareina Yee and María del Mar Martínez, "How Women Can Win in the Workplace," *Harvard Business Review*, March-April 2025, https://hbr.org/2025/03/how-women-can-win-in-the-workplace

46 McKinsey & Company, "Women in the Workplace 2024."

47 McKinsey & Company, "Women in the Workplace 2024."

48 McKinsey & Company, "Women in the Workplace 2023," October 5, 2023, pg. 23, https://www.mckinsey.com/featured-insights/diversity-and-inclusion/women-in-the-workplace-2023.

49 "Men, Commit to Mentor Women," *Lean In*, Accessed February 18, 2025, https://leanin.org/mentor-her#!.

50 "2023–2024 Corporate Equality Index," Human Rights Campaign Foundation, November 2023, reports.hrc.org/corporate-equality-index-2023.

51 Lewis Carroll, *Alice's Adventures in Wonderland*, (MacMillan, 1865).

52 Foust-Cummings, et al., "Sponsoring Women."

Index

www.ingramcontent.com/pod-product-compliance
Lightning Source LLC
Chambersburg PA
CBHW031943190326
41519CB00007B/633